Intelligent Business

Coursebook

Pre-Intermediate
Business English

| Christine Johnson |

Pearson Education Limited
Edinburgh Gate
Harlow
Essex CM20 2JE
England
and Associated Companies throughout the world.

www.longman.com

First published 2006
Second impression 2007

ISBN: 978-0-582-84801-6

Set in Economist Roman 10.5 / 12.5

Printed in Spain by Graficas Estella

Acknowledgements

The author would like to thank the editors, Stephen Nicholl, Bernie Hayden and Clare Nielsen-Marsh for their excellent help and support; and also the following people and organisations for their valuable contributions: Irene Foster, Paul Gardner, Gavin Floyd, Paul Saunders, Nikki Lambert and the Virgin Mobile Marketing team, and the staff and students of LTS Training & Consulting, Bath.

The publishers would like to thank the following people for their helpful comments on the manuscript for this book: Louise Bulloch, Intercom Language Services GmbH; Steve Bush, The British Institute, Florence; William Cooley, Open Schools of Languages, Madrid; Peter Dunn, Groupe ESC, Dijon, Bourgogne; Jolanta Korc-Migoñ, Warsaw University of Technology, Louise Pile; UK.

The publishers would like to thank the following people for their help in piloting and developing this course: Irene Barrall, UK; Richard Booker and Karen Ngeow, University of Hong Kong; Adolfo Escuder, EU Estudios Empresariales, University of Zaragoza; Wendy Farrar, Università Cattolica del Sacro Cuore, Piacenza; Andrew Hopgood, Linguarama, Hamburg; Ann-Marie Hadzima, Dept of Foreign Languages, National Taiwan University, Taiwan; Samuel C. M. Hsieh, English Department, Chinese Culture University, Taipei; Laura Lewis, ABS International, Buenos Aires; Maite Padrós, Universitat de Barcelona; Giuliete Aymard Ramos Siqueira, São Paulo; Richmond Stroupe, World Language Center, Soka University, Tokyo; Michael Thompson, Centro Linguistico Università Commerciale L. Bocconi, Milan; Krisztina Tüll, Európai Nyelvek Stúdiója, Budapest.

The publishers are grateful to The Economist for permission to adapt copyright material on pages 17 (© 2003), 35 (© 2004), 61 (© 2004), 69 (© 2004), 87 (© 2003), 90 (© 2003), 103 (© 2004), 113 (© 2004), 129 (© 2000). All articles copyright of The Economist Newspaper Limited. All rights reserved.

We are also grateful to the following for permission to reproduce copyright material:

BBC News Online for permission to reproduce extracts adapted from "Office workers 'admit to being rude' " 9 June 2004 and 'Modern gadgets raise work stress' 3 June 2004 published on news.bbc.co.uk; BBC News Online and Lynn Robson for permission to reproduce an extract from 'Move over game boys' by Emma Smith published on news.bbc.co.uk; NI Syndication Limited for an extract adapted from 'Turning a healthy passion into pure undiluted profit' by Zoe Brennan published on business.timesonline.co.uk 21 June 2004 © NI Syndication, London 2004; Guardian News Services Limited for an extract adapted from 'When the right job puts you on the road to cheap cover' by Sean Coughlan published in The Guardian 14 August 2004 © Guardian Newspapers Limited 2004; and Kogan Page for extracts taken from The Leaders Guide to Lateral Thinking Skills by Paul Sloane published by Kogan Page 2003.

In some instances we have been unable to trace the owners of copyright material and we would appreciate any information that would enable us to do so.

Photograph acknowledgements

The Publishers are grateful to the following for their permission to reproduce copyright photographs:

Advertising Archives: pg 37; AKG-Images: pg 119; Alamy: pg 8 (tr) (David Crausby), pg 11 (t) (Image 100), pg 11 (b) (Image 100), pg 34 (bl) (Hugh Threlfall), pg 38 (m) (ImageDJ), pg 44 (Mark Boulton), pg 53 (b) (Photofusion Picture Library), pg 65 (Blend Images), pg 70 (Joseph Lawrence Name), pg 87 (Photofusion Picture Library), pg 92 (t) (The Photolibrary, Wales), pg 107 (Dynamic Graphics Group/IT Stock Free), pg 134 (t) (Image State); AOL: pg 8 (ml); Canon UK Ltd: pg 80; CapitalOne: pg 129; Rick Chapman: p 100; Corbis: pg 9 (Tim Pannell), pg 24 (Royalty Free), pg 27 (m) (Roger Ressmeyer), pg 27 (r) (Simon Warren), pg 36 (Frank Trapper), pg 45 (Jose Luis Pelaez, Inc), pg 59 (Jose Fuste Raga), pg 68 (t) (LWA-Dann Tardif), pg 81 (Owen Franken), pg 101 (Royalty Free), pg 111 (Terry W Eggers); Dartington Crystal: pg 116; Digital Stock: pg 128 (Diversity in Business CD); DK Images: pg 27 (l) (Michael Moran), pg 38 (l) (Judith Miller Archives/Somlo Antiques), pg 120 (l) (Kim Taylor & Jane Burton); eBay Inc: pg 22 (t); The Economist: pg 90; Empics: pg 127 (AP/Keystone/Peter Lauth); European Pressphoto Agency: pg 33; Getty: pg 7, pg 8 (bl), pg 8 br, pg 39(m), pg 39(r), p 47, 53 (t), pg 56, pg 85, pg 92 (b), pg 99, pg 106; Goldcorp Inc: pg 126 (t), pg 126 (b); IKEA: pg 34 (tr), pg 137; Image State: pg 68 (b) (First Light); Katz Pictures: pg 61 (FSP); Kos Picture Source: pg 76; London Marriott Hotel Grosvenor Square: pg 103; Microsoft®: pg 8 (mb); Monster.com: pg 67, pg 69; NASA: pg 49 (Marshall Space Flight Center), pg 50 (r) (Johnson Space Center); Gary Neill: pg 15; Nespresso: pg 78; Nokia: pg 34 (tl); Panos: pg 22 (b) (Chris Stowers); PC World: pg 39 (t); © Pearson Education Ltd by Gareth Boden: pg 77; Philips Design: pg 55; PhotoDisc: pg 82 (mobile phone); P J Smoothie: pg 43; Punchstock: pg 12 (Digital Vision), pg 16 (tl) (Rubberball), pg 16 (tr) (Bananastock), pg 16 (b) (Brand X), pg 17 (Digital Vision), pg 21 (l) (PhotoDisc Green), pg 21 (r) (Creatas), pg 41 (Stockbyte), pg 50 (m) (Comstock), pg 63 (Bananastock), pg 73 (Bananastock), pg 74 (Digital Vision), pg 79 (Digital Vision), pg 89 (Bananastock), pg 94 (Image Source), pg 96 (Comstock), pg 105 (Image Source), pg 108 (Image Source), pg 117 (PhotoAlto), pg 118, (Image 100), pg 120 (r) (Digital Vision), pg 125 (Image Source), pg 132 (Bananastock), pg 134 (b) (Digital Vision); © Purestock: pg 25; Red Bull: pg 75 (Richie Hopson); Rex: pg 8 (mt), pg 30, pg 34 (tm), pg 34 (ml), pg 34 (br), 35, 38 (r); Brett Ryder: pg 113; Salty Dog Crisps: pg 46; Science Photo Library: pg 50 (l) (NASA), pg 121; Sony UK: pg 8 (tl); Superstock: pg 48 (Age Fotostock), pg 133 (Good Shoot); Virgin Mobile: pg 82 (logo); Zefa: pg 39 (l) (A Inden).

Front cover images supplied by Getty (left), Goldcorp Inc (centre) and Punchstock (Comstock) (right).

Contents images supplied by European Pressphoto Agency (top left), Monster.com (bottom left) and Corbis (Royalty Free) (right). Page 5 supplied by Empics (AP/Keystone/Peter Lauth).

Picture Research by Hilary Luckcock.

Every effort has been made to trace the copyright holders and we apologise in advance for any unintentional omissions. We would be pleased to insert the appropriate acknowledgement in any subsequent edition of this publication.

Illustration acknowledgements

Kathy Baxendale for 14, 86, 91, 110, 139, 143 and 146; John Bradley 124; Jacey at Debut Art 18 and 72; Kevin Kallaugher (KAL) for 23, 93, 97 and 102; Richard Morris 61, 66 and 114; John Stainton for 40 and 50.

Project managed by Bernie Hayden.

Contents

Image
Fashion's favourite
What is the point of fashion shows? They are very expensive and few people want to buy the dresses, which may cost $100,000 or more. But a show generates a lot of publicity and helps to sell cheaper products with the same brand name. Fashion is big business and brings economic benefit to many. **Page 35.**

Job-seeking
The online job-market
Lots of people now use the internet to find jobs. The biggest online job-search site is monster.com, founded by Jeff Taylor. The monster image and Jeff Taylor's unusual ideas for marketing have made the company a huge success. It not only offers a fast and efficient service but is fun to use as well. **Page 60.**

Service
Getting better service
Americans complain more than the British and, as a result, it seems they get better service. British companies don't get much feedback from their customers, so they don't know what they should do to improve service and often perform badly. American companies have developed better systems for dealing with complaints. **Page 103.**

Intelligent Business
Style guide

Pre-Intermediate
Business English

Learning to write well in a foreign language is one of the most difficult challenges facing the language learner. This pocket-sized style guide will help you find the right words, use an appropriate style and write effectively. **See inside the back cover.**

Bookmap

Motivation

The kids are all right

Many companies, especially in the US, now offer games and sports facilities to attract young people to work for them. They want a younger workforce because the young learn faster and can accept change more easily. In the past, older people took all the decisions, but now young workers often have a lot of responsibility. It means that there is more opportunity to have fun and to achieve success early in your working life.
Page 129.

I have taught English in companies around Europe for many years, so I know how important it is to learn the language of business. As the workplace is becoming more and more international, it is increasingly important for people to learn business English if they want to succeed. But in addition to the language, it is important to be familiar with key business concepts and developments, and to understand how business works in different cultures. *The Economist* magazine is a unique resource which provides extensive coverage of news, current trends and the latest ideas from around the world. I am delighted to have had the opportunity to write *Intelligent Business* in partnership with *The Economist*.

Key business concepts

For the pre-intermediate Coursebook, I have tried to select topics which cover general business areas such as marketing, human resources and production. But I have also chosen topics that reflect the changing world of work: working across international borders, office etiquette and motivation, for example. Finally, I have included one or two more specialist areas such as insurance and technology, which have an important role to play in the business world. The result, I hope, is to give a unique overview of business today as well as providing something of interest to everyone. Students will be able to learn more about the business world and, at the same time, see how key language (both spoken and written) is used in real contexts.

Language development

Each unit has a central theme. Exercises and practical activities are developed around this to practise the key grammar and vocabulary areas. The *Career Skills* pages develop language for communication, and also present students with useful strategies that will help them to be more effective in the workplace. At the end of each unit is a *Dilemma* – a problem-solving activity which consolidates and recycles what has been learned.

The *Intelligent Business* pre-intermediate Coursebook is accompanied by a separate Workbook that provides comprehensive self-study language practice. There is also the *Intelligent Business* pre-intermediate Skills Book: a task-driven intensive course that practises language from the *Intelligent Business* syllabus through authentic business tasks. All of these components are covered by a single Teacher's Book.

People using the Coursebook and the Skills Book can visit the www.intelligent-business.org website which contains further information on the course, downloadable resources, teacher support and premium content from the www.economist.com website.

The aim of *Intelligent Business* is to make a truly contemporary world of business accessible to learners of business English – whatever their level of world and business knowledge. I hope you will also find that it is both enjoyable and beneficial.

I wish you every success in your future English-speaking working lives!

Christine Johnson

Unit 1
Activities

www.longman-elt.com   www.economist.com

Playing the game

Keynotes

Companies have different **activities** and work in different ways. Some companies **manufacture** or **produce goods**, others **provide services**; **retailers** sell goods to the general public. Companies **employ** people to work for them in many kinds of **jobs**. Each person has **responsibility** for a specific area of work and a **role** within the **team** or group that they work with.

What do these companies do? Talk about each company's activities using words from A and B below.

Microsoft designs and sells IT software.

A

create, design, develop, manufacture, market, offer, produce, provide, sell

B

banking services, cars, clothing, electronic goods, food and drink, internet services, IT software

Some companies have a number of different business activities. Read the short text below about General Electric (GE) and answer the questions.

General Electric

GE is a diversified technology, media and financial services company. The company mission statement is to create products that make life better: from aircraft engines to industrial machinery to insurance, medical technology, television news and plastics. GE operates in more than 100 countries and employs more than 300,000 people worldwide.

1 Name two more industry **sectors** mentioned in the text: *Technology …*
2 Name two more things that GE **produces**: *Aircraft engines …*
3 How many people **work for** GE?
4 Which word means that GE has **many different** business activities?

Work with a partner. Think of a company in your country or town. What are its main activities? Does it specialise in one industry sector or is it diversified?

1 Read the article about a company called Frognation. <u>Underline</u> Frognation's activities and put a (circle) round the things that Lynn Robson does in her work.

2 Read the article again. Are these statements true or false?

1 Frognation works on video games that sell in the UK.
2 Lynn works mainly in Tokyo.
3 Frognation does all the production work to prepare the games for the market.
4 Lynn knows a lot about Japanese culture.
5 The video game industry is growing rapidly.
6 Not many women work in the video game industry.

Move over game boys

Lynn Robson is a co-founder of Frognation. The company creates soundtracks and designs and translates Japanese video games for the UK market. With her partners in Tokyo and her international team of designers and developers, Lynn creates the video games that thousands are playing today.

Lynn runs the UK office of Frognation, while her two business partners run the Tokyo office. Her Japanese computer system, and, of course, email make it possible to work across borders and time zones.

Frognation represents producers with great game ideas and helps them to sell their ideas to Sony or Nintendo in Tokyo. Once the games go into development, Lynn and her team provide advice on everything from the music soundtrack and graphics to the game programming and characters. The result is a new kind of video game, created by artists, which provides exciting game play.

Cultural understanding is important. When she is in meetings in Japan, Lynn gives advice on what will work in both countries. In the West, Lynn becomes the Japan expert, giving clients information about Japanese culture. When her Japanese partners come to meetings in the UK, Lynn helps them to present their ideas in the best way, and tries to avoid any cultural misunderstandings.

Video game sales are sky-rocketing at the moment. There are thousands of opportunities to build careers in the video game industry, but women don't often consider gaming as a career.

Today most video games are created by men, and for men. So it is no surprise that almost all video games are either sports games or shoot-em-ups.

With more women like Lynn joining the video game industry, however, things could change.

Glossary

soundtrack music or other sounds on a video, film, etc.

graphics pictures or images designed for a video game, computer program, etc.

programming writing a computer program

characters the people in a video game, film, etc.

sky-rocketing going up very fast

shoot-em-ups violent games where people shoot and kill each other

1 What do you think are the good things about Lynn Robson's job? What are the bad things?

2 What do you think of video games? Do video games usually appeal more to men and boys than to women and girls? Why?

Vocabulary 1

Roles and activities

Match the words 1–5 with the meanings a–e.

1 founder
2 set up
3 team
4 partner
5 run (a business)

a to start a company or organisation
b one of a number of people who own a business together
c to be responsible for
d a group of people who work together to do a job
e someone who starts a company or organisation

Vocabulary 2

Word building

1 Jobs

What do you call someone who works in each of the following areas?

a technical job – *technician*

1 accounts
2 art
3 banking
4 economics
5 engineering
6 music

2 Job titles

Complete the job titles in the sentences. Use a dictionary if necessary.

A financial _*analyst*_ is someone who **analyses** the financial markets.

1 A financial ________ is someone who gives **advice** about financial services.
2 A sales ________ is someone who **represents** their company and sells their products.
3 An ________ manager is someone who **assists** the manager.
4 A ________ ________ offers **consultancy** services to **management.**
5 A ________ ________ is someone who **develops software.**
6 A ________ ________ is someone who **produces films.**

Present simple and continuous

1 Match the examples with the rules below.

1 Lynn **runs** the office of Frognation.
2 Video game sales **are sky-rocketing** at the moment.
3 Lynn frequently **travels** to Japan for meetings.
4 Lynn **is working** at home this week.

Use the present simple to describe:

a regular or routine activities
b permanent or long-term situations

Use the present continuous to describe:

c something happening now
d a temporary situation

2 Choose the correct alternatives in *italics*.

1 We usually use the present *simple / continuous* with these expressions:
  normally   every day   often   sometimes   frequently
2 We usually use the present *simple / continuous* with these expressions:
  at the moment   now   this week   currently

 For more information, see page 157.

For more information, see page 157.

Practice

1 Choose the correct verb forms in *italics* to complete the text.

We're all accountants and we ¹*work / are working* for a telecommunications company in the finance department. We ²*sit / are sitting* at our PCs in the office every day and ³*check / are checking* the invoices and payments. But this week is different: we ⁴*attend / are attending* a training course. The company ⁵*currently changes / is currently changing* to a new accounting system, and this week, we ⁶*learn / are learning* all about it. So at the moment, we ⁷*stay / are staying* at a big hotel in the mountains. It's wonderful! When we're at home, we usually ⁸*spend / are spending* the evenings cooking and cleaning for our families. But here, there's an excellent restaurant and we can relax and have a laugh together.

2 Complete the text with the correct forms of the verbs in brackets.

My working day (¹start) _____ with a long journey to the office – usually over an hour on a crowded train. The first event of a typical day is the regular morning meeting. Our managers (²give) _____ updates on the department's progress. After that, it's a long, hard day of work. You can see me at work in this photo – I (³give) _____ a presentation to my colleagues. I often (⁴stay) _____ in the office until 9 or 10pm. But this is the old way. Now, things (⁵begin) _____ to change. Young people (⁶refuse) _____ to work long hours. They (⁷demand) _____ more leisure time and freedom.

Speaking

Describe your daily or weekly routine activities to a partner.
Describe any special projects you are working on at the moment, or any special events in your personal life.

How to write emails

1 Anna Davidson, a training manager and expert in business communication, talks about *virtual teams*: international teams which communicate mainly by email. Listen to the first part. What are the advantages and disadvantages of using email to communicate with colleagues in other countries?

2 Which of the following are most important when writing to a colleague in another country? Discuss your ideas with a partner.

- Tell your colleagues about yourself.
- Only write about work.
- Keep your message very short.
- If there is a problem, explain it carefully.
- Use polite phrases.

3 Now listen to the second part of Anna Davidson's talk. Tick the points above which she recommends.

Reading 3   Read two examples of an email from a Japanese designer to his London colleagues about the text for a new webpage. Which one follows Anna Davidson's recommendations?

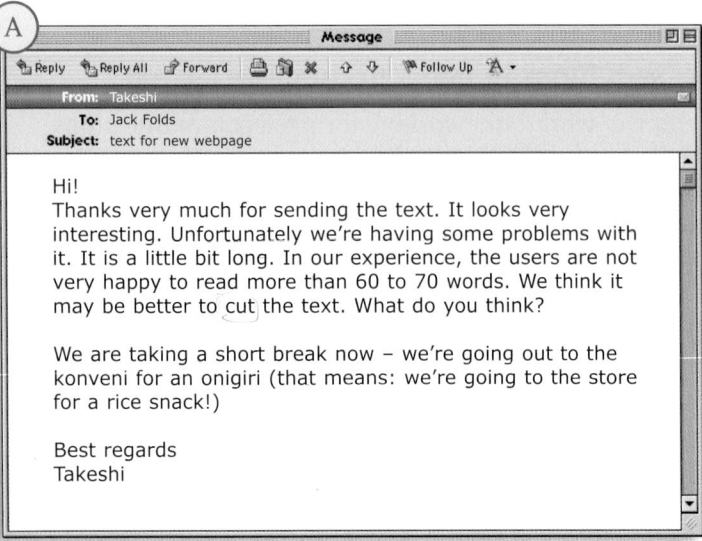

A

From: Takeshi
To: Jack Folds
Subject: text for new webpage

Hi!
Thanks very much for sending the text. It looks very interesting. Unfortunately we're having some problems with it. It is a little bit long. In our experience, the users are not very happy to read more than 60 to 70 words. We think it may be better to cut the text. What do you think?

We are taking a short break now – we're going out to the konveni for an onigiri (that means: we're going to the store for a rice snack!)

Best regards
Takeshi

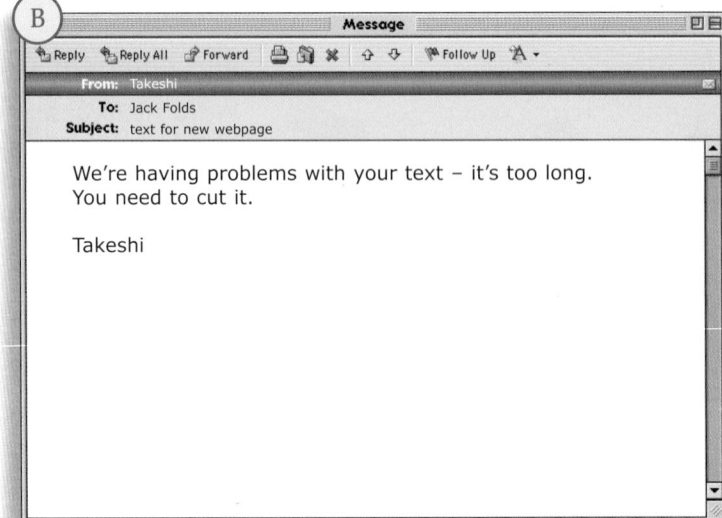

B

From: Takeshi
To: Jack Folds
Subject: text for new webpage

We're having problems with your text – it's too long. You need to cut it.

Takeshi

Writing   Tracey Smith, a colleague in another country, has sent you a sample page for a new website design. You want to make the following comment about it:

There's a problem with the new website design. The colours are too dark. It's difficult to read the text. Tracey needs to find new colours.

Write an email to Tracey Smith. Follow one of the examples above and make the comment more friendly and polite. Decide how to start and end the email. End the message with a little 'conversation' as Takeshi does in Example A above.

Explaining your job

When you introduce yourself, it is common to say something about your job and where you work. Look at the following phrases. Match each phrase with a question a–d.

1   I'm a ... (graphics designer)
2   I work as a ... (consultant)
3   I work for ... (a media company)
4   We provide ... (web design services)
5   I'm responsible for ... (project management / managing projects)
6   My main role is to ... (meet with clients, sell our services)

a   What kind of company do you work for?
b   What does your company do?
c   What do you do in your job?
d   What's your job?

Listening 2

1 Listen to four people explaining their job and job activities. Match the jobs, companies and main activities with the person.

Person	Job	Company	Main activity
Olaf	Lawyer	Paper manufacturer	manages IT systems
Rania	Accountant	Finance house	meets clients
Da The	Project Manager	Mobile phone company	deals with payments
Jaana	Systems Developer	Travel company	checks contracts

2 Listen again. What other activities does each person do?

3 Which of the above phrases does each person use? Tick the phrases you heard. Then listen again and check.

Speaking

1 Imagine you are Olaf, Rania, Da The or Jaana. Introduce yourself to your partner. Explain your job, company and job activities.

2 Work with a partner. You should each choose a different company and job for yourself. Practise asking and answering questions a–d above.

Culture at work

Greeting people

How do you greet a new contact or colleague in your country? In business, do you usually shake hands? When? Is it OK to use first names with someone you don't know? These things may be different in other cultures. Can you give any examples from your own experience?

Dilemma & Decision

Dilemma: Exporting to Mexico

Brief

A British company, Systemax, manufactures and sells laboratory equipment to three main regions: Europe, North America and Asia Pacific. Systemax is entering a new export market in Mexico. Sales in Mexico are small at the moment, but the company expects a big increase in the next two years and hopes to expand further into South America during the next five years. Systemax has two export managers for the main regions:

George Johnstone, North America; Linda McCade, Europe.

Now someone has to take responsibility for exports to Mexico. Is it better to give extra responsibility to George Johnstone or to Linda McCade? Or perhaps the company needs to find a third export manager?

The extra responsibility means travelling to Mexico (and in future, to countries in South America) several times a year and building good relationships with customers there. Mexico has a border with the US and, in terms of geography, could be part of the North America region. But its culture is very different from the US culture. It is in many ways more similar to the culture of Spain.

You are the Systemax directors and have to decide. Consider:

- What abilities and experience do George and Linda have?
- How much time does each have for extra responsibilities?
- Are they ready to increase the amount of travel abroad?

Task 1

Work in two groups. Look for the answers to the three questions above.

Group A: Find out more about George Johnstone. Turn to page 137.

Group B: Find out more about Linda McCade. Turn to page 140.

Task 2

Work in new groups of 4–6. Half of each group should be from Group A and half from Group B. Tell the others what information you have about George Johnstone or Linda McCade. Discuss the information and decide if it is a good idea to give extra responsibility to either George or Linda. Or you may decide to look for a third export manager.

Write it up

Write an email to either George Johnstone or Linda McCade, offering him/her the job and explaining why. Use these words in your email:

I'm writing to tell you that we would like to offer you the job of ...

We think you are the right person for this job because ...

Decision:

Listen to Alistair Cross, a director of Systemax. Alistair explains the company's decision regarding responsibility for exports to Mexico.

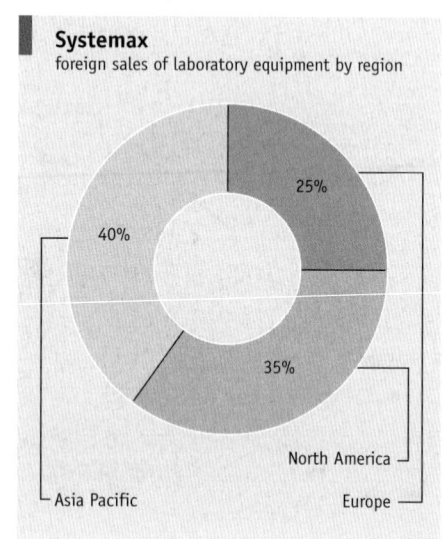

Systemax
foreign sales of laboratory equipment by region

25%
40%
35%

North America
Asia Pacific
Europe

Unit 2
Data

www.longman-elt.com   www.economist.com

No privacy

Keynotes

Information technology (IT) makes it easy to **store** huge amounts of **data**, or information, on **computer databases**. Companies and organisations **collect** information about people all the time. Companies **conduct research** into people's **buying habits** so that they can improve their marketing. Organisations collect data for **surveillance** purposes: to help stop criminal activity and increase **security**. Someone somewhere is **recording** nearly everything we do.

Why do companies collect data? What kind of data do they collect?

Companies collect market research data to improve their marketing.

1 **Listen to three people who have to collect and manage data in their work. Match the people 1–3 with what they do a–c.**

1	Amy	a	searches for information on the internet
2	Bob	b	stores records in a database
3	Carla	c	writes market research reports

2 **Listen again and answer the questions.**

1 Why is it useful to collect information about customers' buying habits?
2 What are the three questions Bob has to answer in his work?
3 Who uses Bob's reports?
4 What is Carla's job and what does she try to do?
5 Does Carla always use the same suppliers?

3 **Complete the sentences with these words. Listen and check.**

browse	enters	keeps	manages	uses	updates

1 Amy _manages_ customer data and _____ records of customers.
2 She _____ data in the customer database.
3 Bob collects data about people who _____ the company website.
4 Carla _____ search engines to find new products and suppliers.
5 She _____ the files with new information.

Companies can now collect detailed information about us. Which of these things are you happy about? Are they necessary?

1 Other people can read your emails.
2 Mobile phone companies can monitor your calls.
3 Video cameras in the street film you.
4 Companies collect details of your shopping habits.
5 Airlines can check your personal records before you fly.

1 **Read the article on the opposite page quickly and choose the sentence which best summarises the main idea.**

1 New technology is helping to find internet criminals.
2 It is difficult to store a lot of data.
3 Modern life is not very private.

2 **Read the article again and answer the following questions.**

1 How do companies collect information about people who visit websites?
2 How can organisations find out where we go?
3 What are some of the new developments in surveillance technology?
4 What four advantages of surveillance technology are mentioned?
5 What do most people think about having so much surveillance?

The internet society
No hiding place

The protection of privacy will be a huge problem for the internet society

A cookie is a small file that a company can send to your computer when you visit the company's website. It tells them a lot about your browsing habits. Using the web without them is nearly impossible. DoubleClick, an advertising company, has agreements with over 11,000 websites and maintains cookies on 100 million users to get information about them for marketing.

Offline, the story is the same. When you turn on a mobile phone, the phone company can monitor calls and also record the location of the phone. We use more and more electronic systems for tickets, and for access to buildings. It is becoming common for employers to monitor employees' telephone calls, voicemail, email and computer use.

The use of video surveillance cameras is also growing. Britain has about 1.5 million cameras in public places (for example, airports, shopping malls and public buildings). The average Briton is recorded by CCTV cameras 300 times a day. With digital cameras we can collect, store and analyse millions of images.

And this is only the beginning. Engineers are now developing cameras that can "see" through clothing, walls or cars. Satellites can recognise objects only one metre across. We can attach tracking chips to products or people.

New technology offers substantial benefits – more security against terrorists and criminals, higher productivity at work, a wider selection of products, more convenience. We are ready to give more personal information because we want the benefits.

But all this monitoring generates a mountain of data about us. Surveillance is everywhere in our society, often without our knowledge. Most people hate the idea but they don't know how to stop it. ■

Glossary

CCTV cameras closed circuit television cameras – police and security staff can watch the film and follow people's movements

tracking chips microchips that use radio signals to find the exact location of someone or something

Speaking **Who do you think benefits most from surveillance? Governments, companies or individuals? What are the dangers of too much surveillance?**

Using the internet

1 Match the words 1–8 with the pictures a–h.

1	website	5	search engine
2	online shopping	6	password
3	screen	7	mouse
4	keyword	8	click

2 Complete the text with a suitable word or phrase from exercise 1.

When you want to find information on the web, it is helpful to use a
¹_____ such as Google or AltaVista. You type in a ²_____ or
phrase, ³_____ on 'GO' and a list of ⁴_____ appears on your
computer ⁵_____ . Many people use the web for ⁶_____ or
banking. This means they have to enter private information such as credit
card numbers or bank details, so the website must be very secure. To enter a
secure site, you usually need to enter your username and a ⁷_____ .

Quantity and number

1 Put the following words and phrases in the correct group.

a bit of	a few	huge	millions	a mountain of
substantial	tiny	wide	enormous	a fraction

Large / a lot	Small / not many

2 Match the numerical expressions 1–5 with the descriptions a–e.

1	0.5	a	frequency, how often something happens
2	1 metre wide	b	a decimal
3	millions (of ...)	c	a fraction
4	300 times a day	d	a huge number – we don't know how many
5	a quarter	e	the size of something

Numbers

Listen to Bob from Listening 1 on page 16 describing a report about his company's website. Write the numbers you hear.

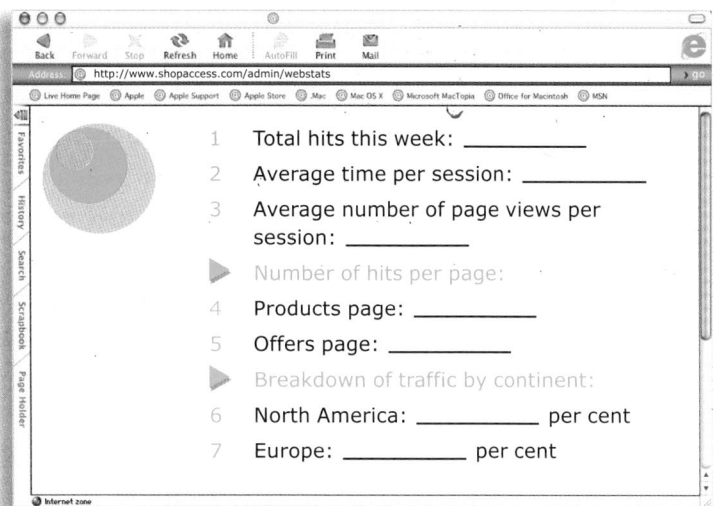

1   Total hits this week: _____
2   Average time per session: _____
3   Average number of page views per session: _____
▶   Number of hits per page:
4   Products page: _____
5   Offers page: _____
▶   Breakdown of traffic by continent:
6   North America: _____ per cent
7   Europe: _____ per cent

Say the numbers. Then listen and check.

1	a	815	b	10,000	c	4,905
2	a	3.2	b	10.98	c	15.361
3	a	⅛	b	⅓	c	²/₇
4	a	2%	b	48%	c	91.3%
5	a	£102	b	4,000 USD	c	€9m

1 Listen to Sandra Ravell giving advice on how to manage data and answer the questions.

1   She names three kinds of people who need to manage large amounts of information. Who are they?
2   Why is it important to manage information well?

2 Listen again and complete the notes with the missing words.

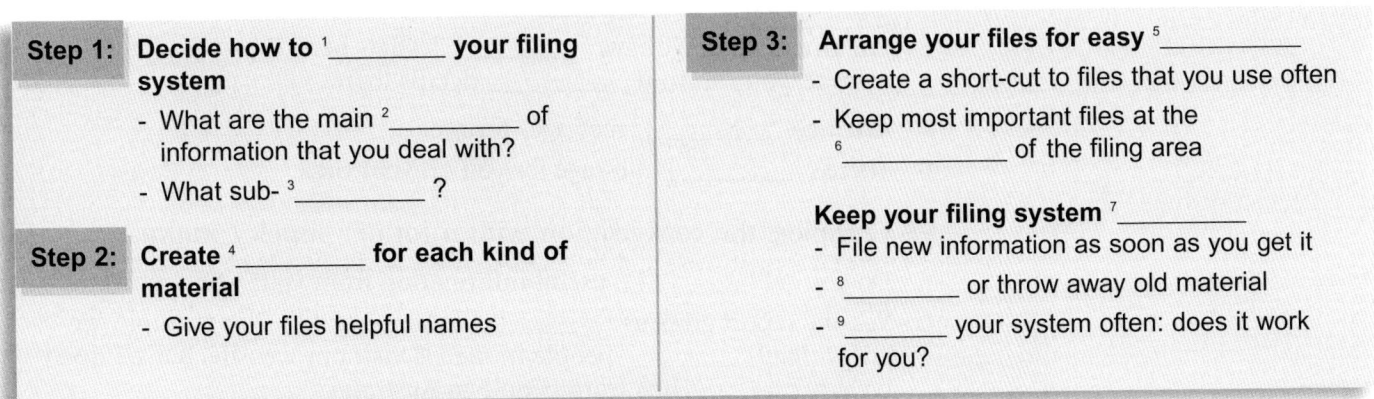

Step 1: Decide how to ¹_____ your filing system
- What are the main ²_____ of information that you deal with?
- What sub-³_____?

Step 2: Create ⁴_____ for each kind of material
- Give your files helpful names

Step 3: Arrange your files for easy ⁵_____
- Create a short-cut to files that you use often
- Keep most important files at the ⁶_____ of the filing area

Keep your filing system ⁷_____
- File new information as soon as you get it
- ⁸_____ or throw away old material
- ⁹_____ your system often: does it work for you?

Work with a partner. Tell each other what systems you use for recording and storing English vocabulary.

Countable and uncountable

1 **Which of the following nouns in bold are countable (C) and which are uncountable (U)?**

a Do you have any **statistics** on web users?

b We have a lot of **information** about shopping on the internet.

c Some **people** dislike shopping on the internet.

d Do you have many **customers** in the US?

e We don't have much **time** to analyse all the data.

f Do you use much **surveillance equipment** in your company?

g There's a **camera** in reception.

h We can't give you any **advice** on security.

i The company doesn't have any **problems** with security.

j This website doesn't have many **pages**.

2 **Match the sentences above with the rules. Write** *countable nouns,* *uncountable nouns* **or** *both.*

Positive sentences	Negative sentences	Questions
Use *a* or *any* with singular ¹_____ .	Use *any* with ⁴_____ and with ⁵_____ in the plural.	Use *any* with uncountable nouns and ⁸_____ in the plural.
Use *some* with all uncountable nouns and with ²_____ in the plural.	Use *much* with ⁶_____ .	Use *much* with ⁹_____ .
Use *a lot of* with ³_____ .	Use *many* with ⁷_____ .	Use *many* with ¹⁰_____ .

Note: In offers and requests, we usually use *some,* not *any.*

Can you bring me some water? (request) *Would you like some coffee?* (offer)

For more information, see page 157.

1 **Complete the conversations with** *a / some / any.*

A Can you send me ¹_____ information about the hotel, please?

B I'm afraid we don't have ²_____ leaflets here. If you go to their website, you can find ³_____ details there.

A Are there ⁴_____ messages for me?

B There's ⁵_____ message for you on your desk.

2 **Complete the conversation with** *a lot of / much / many.*

A Do you get ¹_____ useful information from your web report?

B Yes, the report gives us ²_____ interesting data. For example, we know that ³_____ people in the US visit our website. But we don't have ⁴_____ hits from people in Australia.

Work with a partner. Ask questions about a region, town or company that he/she knows. Answer your partner's questions.

How many people live in … ? Are there any good restaurants?

Checking information

Numbers are everywhere in business. Sometimes it is important to listen and write down a precise number. You need to check that you have got the number correct, especially on the telephone. Here are some useful expressions for checking:

Sorry – I didn't catch that.

Can you repeat it, please?

Did you say ... ?

Do you mean ... ?

Sorry, can I just check ... ?

Sorry – did you say ... ?

Sometimes it is enough to give approximate numbers. For example, we can say:

about half a million   **just under** a thousand   **over** two million

Listening 5

1 **Listen to two people talking about internet statistics on the phone. Write the precise or approximate numbers you hear.**

1   Number of people online worldwide: _____

2   Percentage of people online in Europe: _____

3   Number of people online in Europe: _____

4   Time each person spends browsing: _____

2 **Listen again. Tick the expressions from the list above that speaker A uses to check the figures.**

Speaking

Work in pairs. You are going to give each other some customer data. Student A give Student B this information. Write the information that Student B gives you. Student B turn to page 140.

Name: Jane Doe   Age: 35

Salary: $69,950 a year

Car: expects to spend $18,000 on next car

Drives 15,400 kilometres a year

Works in a company with 1,568 employees

Spends 1.4% of salary on clothes

Culture at work

Are you precise or approximate?

If someone asks you the time, do you give a precise answer (for example, 'It's two minutes past ten') or an approximate answer ('Ten o'clock')? In some cultures, people think it is important to give precise numbers. These things are not so important in other cultures.

Dilemma & Decision

Dilemma: Buy it now!

Brief

eBay, the online auction site, wants to expand. The best way is to set up operations in other countries like India. It has over a billion people and could be the biggest market in the world in the future. But how many people there have access to the internet? Are they ready for online shopping? Are there other online auction companies? How easy is it for a foreign company to enter the market?

eBay is asking you, a group of market researchers, to find out about India. Should eBay enter the market in India?

Task 1

Work in small groups. What information do you need to help eBay make its decision? Look at the areas below and prepare a list of questions.

1   Access to the internet – numbers?

How many people have access to the internet in India?

2   Where (home, school, internet café)?

3   Who (students, young professionals, families ...)?

4   For what purpose (email, shopping, entertainment ...)?

5   Technical problems (connections, phone lines)?

6   Paying for goods (credit cards)?

7   Competition (from other online auction companies in India)?

Task 2

Work in two groups. Find out the answers to some of the questions in Task 1. Group A turn to page 137. Group B turn to page 140.

Task 3

Work in new groups of 4–6. Half of each group should be from Group A and half from Group B. Practise asking and answering your questions.

Task 4

Now discuss the information you found out in Task 3. Is it a good idea for eBay to set up operations in India or not?

Write it up

Write the **conclusion** of a market report for eBay, which gives the findings of the market research on India. In your conclusion, give your decision and explain the reasons for it.

Conclusion:

Taking all these facts into consideration, we believe that the best decision is ... because ...

Decision:

⊙ Now listen to Deepak Gupta, an expert in e-commerce in India, explaining the decision that eBay took.

Useful phrases

How many people ... ?

Where do they usually ... ?

Do they ... ?

Is there any ... ?

Are there any ... ?

Unit 3 Etiquette

www.longman-elt.com   www.economist.com

Bad manners at work

Keynotes

Etiquette is the name we give to the **rules** for being **polite** in a social group. Business etiquette is important for people who often have to make new **contacts** and **build relationships** in their work. **Politeness** can also help to **improve** the **working environment** for people in the same office. Some cultures and situations are **formal**, which means that we have to follow rules; other cultures and situations are more **informal**.

Politeness at work

1 Discuss these examples of bad manners. Which ones do you think are especially bad? Why?

- arriving late for a meeting
- ignoring people when you meet them
- shouting an order at someone
- not apologising if you offend someone
- being rude to people who offer to help you
- using bad language

2 What other examples of good or bad manners can you think of? Work in small groups and make two lists. Then compare your lists with other groups. Do you all have the same opinions about politeness?

Listening 1 ⊙

1 Janet Stubbs, a professor of communication, talks about politeness in the workplace. Listen to part one and complete what she says.

Politeness is about showing _____ for others.

It means thinking about other people's _____ .

2 Listen to part two and answer the questions.

1 Who are we usually polite to in a business environment? Give two examples.

2 Why is it better if managers show respect for their workers?

3 Complete the extracts with words from the box. Then listen to part two again and check.

| hierarchy | rules | status | subordinates |

1 In formal situations, it is a good idea to follow standard _____ when making new contacts.

2 Politeness is often linked to _____ .

3 We are more polite to people who are above us in the organisational _____ .

Reading **1** Read the article on the opposite page and find six examples of bad manners. Which three examples of bad manners is the company in the article trying to stop?

2 **Read the article again and answer the following questions.**

1 What reason do office workers give for their bad manners?
2 Why is it impolite to answer a mobile phone during a meeting?
3 Are people today more polite than they were 20 years ago?
4 What are some organisations doing to improve workers' manners?
5 What are the benefits of avoiding bad manners at work?

Office workers 'admit being rude'

MOST office workers say they are rude or bad-mannered at work. Two out of three workers regularly arrive late for meetings, most ignore emails and three out of four use bad language. In a survey of 1,000 workers, two-thirds say that pressure of work is the reason for their bad manners.

Other common examples of bad office etiquette include ignoring colleagues and answering mobile phone calls during meetings. Using mobile phones in meetings is impolite and distracts others, research by the University of Surrey shows. If you respond to a call when speaking to somebody, it means that the phone call is more important than the person, the survey said. If you answer a call during a meeting, it could mean that you think the meeting is not important.

Mr Jacobs, managing director of Office Angels, a recruitment firm, says it is easy for people to forget their manners in the working environment, which is often very informal and very busy. Workers can forget proper etiquette such as introducing people at meetings, and this is often bad for working relationships.

Psychologist Dr Colin Gill believes that people are not as polite as they were twenty years ago. He said: 'Courtesy is no longer something that is so much respected in our society.' People think it is 'stuffy to be polite or formal.'

Now some organisations are actually investing money in training their junior managers to be polite. Office Angels is encouraging people to arrive on time for meetings, turn off mobile phones and avoid bad language. 'Avoiding bad manners at work is such a simple thing to do,' Mr Jacobs says, 'and it can have a dramatic impact on improving your working environment and your relationships with others.'

Glossary

distract stop people paying attention

stuffy old fashioned, boring, not friendly

Speaking 1 **Do you have experience of the bad manners described in the article? How do you feel when other people show bad manners?**

2 **Do you agree that 'courtesy is no longer respected' and 'it's stuffy to be polite'? Why? / Why not?**

Complete the text with these words from the article.

| admit | avoid | ignore | introduce | invest |
| improve | respond | | | |

A recruitment firm gives this advice to new workers:

It is important to [1]_____ time in your relationships with others at work. Get to know the people who work near you: [2]_____ yourself to them and tell them something about yourself. If people ask for your help, always [3]_____ positively. Don't [4]_____ emails or phone calls just because you are busy. If you make a mistake, it is better to [5]_____ it and then apologise. When things go wrong, stay calm and [6]_____ shouting and using bad language. Remember, good manners help to [7]_____ your working environment, and you will find you can enjoy your work more.

Synonyms

Look at the following groups of words. Which word does not belong in each group?

1   rude, stuffy, bad-mannered, impolite
2   courtesy, politeness, etiquette, impact
3   communicate, answer, reply, respond
4   regularly, commonly, rarely, often

Prefixes

1 **Add the following prefixes to the adjectives below to make words with the opposite meaning. Use a dictionary if necessary.**

| un- | in- | dis- | im- |

1 formal	4 polite	7 friendly	10 respectful
2 satisfied	5 practical	8 efficient	11 patient
3 honest	6 considerate	9 important	12 appropriate

2 **Use words from exercise 1 to complete the definitions.**

Someone who is bad-mannered is _impolite_ .

Someone who ...
1   ... doesn't tell the truth is _____ .
2   ... wants to do things in a hurry and finish quickly is _____ .
3   ... doesn't like other people and doesn't want to talk is _____ .
4   ... works slowly and doesn't do their job well is _____ .
5   ... doesn't think about other people's needs or wishes is _____ .
6   ... isn't happy with the way things happened is _____ .

Business etiquette in other cultures

1 Listen to three people describing business etiquette in their cities – Sydney, London and New York – and answer the questions.

In which city ...
1 ... do people like to be informal?
2 ... are people very competitive?
3 ... are things changing?

2 Listen again, make notes and complete the table.

	Sydney	London	New York
Breakfast meetings	common – 8am		
Punctuality		important	
Dress			
Lunch			
What do people talk about outside work?			business

Speaking **1** Are business people in your country easy-going or more formal? What do they usually wear to work?

2 Do most business people in your country have a long lunch at a restaurant or do they eat a quick sandwich?

Writing Write an email to a friend in Sydney, London or New York who is planning to come to your country on business. Look at the information in the table above. Tell him or her about any practices that are different in your two countries.

Offers and requests

1 Tick the most informal expression in each group below.

2 Tick the responses that mean 'no'. What words do we sometimes use to avoid saying 'no'?

Offers	Responses
Can I help you?	Yes, I'm looking for Mr Jones.
Let me carry your bags for you.	Thanks – that's very kind of you.
Would you like a coffee?	Not just now, thanks.
Do you want some sugar?	I don't take sugar, thanks.
I could make a copy for you.	Thanks, but I don't really need one.

Requests	Responses
Can you phone me tomorrow?	It's a bit difficult. I'm very busy.
Could I have some water, please?	Yes, of course.
Would you please check the figures?	Yes, no problem.
Could you give me some directions, please?	I'm sorry. I don't know this place very well.

For more information, see page 158.

Practice 1 **Choose the most appropriate words in *italics*.**

1 *Can I / I want* to see the photos?
2 *Do you want that I / Can I* help you with your bags?
3 *Could I / Let me* borrow your magazine to read?
4 *Could you / Would you like* to sit down?
5 *Would I / Could I* have some more milk, please?
6 *You could / Could you* open the door for me, please?
7 *Can you / Please* give me your phone number?

Listening 3 Rising intonation ⤴ is more polite for requests and offers. Falling intonation ⤵ sounds like an order. Listen to six examples. Decide if each one is a request (R) or an order (O).

1 _____ 2 _____ 3 _____ 4 _____ 5 _____ 6 _____

Practice 2 **How could you refuse these offers and requests politely, without using the word 'no'? Discuss your ideas with a partner.**

1 Can I phone you at 10 o'clock tonight?
2 Would you like to try some of our English beer?
3 Could you give me your report today, please?
4 Let me show you around our factory.
5 Could you tell me about the history of your town?
6 Do you want a lift to the airport?

Speaking **1** Work in pairs. You are going to ask each other for help. Student A turn to page 137. Student B turn to page 141.

2 Role-play similar situations with your partner.

Being polite

Match the polite phrases 1–6 with the replies a–f.

1	Can I introduce my colleague? This is Jane Duncan.	a	No problem. You're welcome.
2	I'm really sorry about my mistake.	b	That would be very nice. Thank you!
3	Thanks very much for your help.	c	That's all right. Don't worry about it.
4	Would you like to join us for lunch?	d	I'm glad you enjoyed it.
5	Is it OK to smoke in here?	e	Pleased to meet you.
6	Thanks for a very nice lunch.	f	I'm sorry. It isn't allowed.

Listening 4 ⊙

1 **Listen to six short conversations. How does the second person reply in each situation? Choose the correct description in *italics*.**

1 John points out a mistake. Jane *apologises / doesn't apologise* for it.

2 Jack invites Barbara to dinner. Barbara *accepts / refuses* the invitation.

3 John introduces Caroline Day to Barbara. Barbara *knows / doesn't know* her.

4 Jack asks if he is allowed to park in front of the office. Jane says that he *can / can't*.

5 Barbara gives Jane a gift. Jane *likes / doesn't like* it.

6 Jack helped John to arrange his travel. It *was / wasn't* a problem for Jack.

2 **Listen again and underline the phrases in the table above that the speakers use.**

Speaking **Work in small groups. Take turns to role-play the following situations:**

1 A business partner from the UK comes to visit you in your office. Introduce your colleagues.

2 Invite your visitor to a local football match this evening.

3 You are the visitor. You want to know if you can smoke in the office.

4 Your colleague helped you to prepare the conference room for a meeting. Say thank you.

5 You spill coffee on a document that your colleague is reading. Apologise.

6 You are a visitor from abroad. Your business partner takes you to the airport to catch your flight home. Say thank you.

Culture at work ## Being direct

When you make requests in your country, do you use a lot of polite phrases, or do you just say directly what you want? In some cultures, people prefer to be direct. For example, they may go into a restaurant and say: 'I want to see the menu!' In other cultures, people think it is impolite to be so direct. They might say: 'Do you think we could possibly have a look at the menu, please?'

Dilemma & Decision

Dilemma: A workplace bully

Brief

Elizabeth works for a computer company. At first, she liked the job and believed that she could do it well. But now she has a problem: her team leader, Valma, is a bully. Valma seems to dislike Elizabeth. She always finds problems with her work. If Elizabeth makes a small mistake, she shouts at her in front of her colleagues: 'What's wrong with you? Are you stupid?' She doesn't talk to the other team members in this way. She gives Elizabeth all the most boring and difficult tasks to do. Elizabeth wants to go on a training course. She wants to specialise and be able to do more interesting work. But Valma always finds a reason to stop her. She tells her she has no ability. Elizabeth feels tired and stressed. She is starting to believe that she really is stupid. What should Elizabeth do?

She has four options:

- talk to her colleagues about it
- talk to Valma herself
- report the bullying to a senior manager in the company
- leave the job

Task 1

To find a good solution, it is helpful to understand why someone is a bully. There are three main types of bully. Read about one of these types. Work in three groups. Group A turn to page 141. Group B turn to page 143. Group C turn to page 144.

Task 2

Form groups of three: one person from each group, A, B and C above. Take turns to describe one type of bully to your partners. Which description do you think best matches Valma? Using the information about this type of bully, decide on the best option for Elizabeth. Of course, she can try more than one option. But which one is not such a good solution? Why?

Write it up

Write a friendly email to Elizabeth. Explain why you think Valma is bullying Elizabeth. Tell her what she should do.

Decision:

⊙ Now listen to Gary Robinson, a business psychologist, giving his opinion about Elizabeth's situation.

Review 1

Language check

Present simple and continuous

Complete the sentences with the correct form of the present simple or continuous.

1 Mark is a market research assistant: he (analyse) _____ market data.

2 Today is a holiday and Mark isn't in the office. He (play) _____ football.

3 Mark (play) _____ football twice a week.

4 Currently, Mark and his colleagues (work) _____ on a special project.

5 They (conduct) _____ market research for a new sports magazine called *Goal!*

6 Young men (read) _____ the magazine.

7 *Goal!* has a problem at the moment: Not many people (buy) _____ the magazine.

8 Mark thinks that this is because men (not read) _____ magazines very often.

some / any / a / much / many / a lot of

Complete the text with the best option a–c.

Nowadays, [1]_____ people are rich. But the rich aren't always happy. People who have [2]_____ money don't want to be without it, but they can have [3]_____ big problems sometimes. They often don't have [4]_____ close relationships.

Sports stars and entertainers may have [5]_____ hard life because they spend [6]_____ time away from friends and family. Twenty-nine-year-olds in Silicon Valley who don't need to work any more often feel that there isn't [7]_____ purpose to their life. It may sound strange, but there aren't [8]_____ young people who want to spend their whole life playing games.

1	a	a lot of	b	much	c	any
2	a	many	b	much	c	a lot of
3	a	any	b	some	c	much
4	a	some	b	many	c	much
5	a	some	b	any	c	a
6	a	a lot of	b	many	c	any
7	a	a	b	some	c	many
8	a	much	b	many	c	some

Offers and requests

Which offer or request 1–6 matches both responses a–f?

1 Would you like a drink?

2 Let me show you our new offices.

3 Can I post your letters for you?

4 Could you give me Jon's number, please?

5 Would you please bring me some tea?

6 Could I use your office this afternoon?

a That would be nice, but I haven't got much time, I'm afraid.
   Thank you. That would be very interesting.

b I'm sorry, we haven't got any.
   Yes, of course.

c Sorry. I haven't got it.
   Yes. Just a moment, it's on the database.

d Not just now, thanks.
   Just a glass of water, please.

e It's a bit difficult. Jackie's using it.
   Yes, that's no problem.

f Don't worry, I can do it myself.
   Oh, thanks very much!

Consolidation

Choose the correct words in *italics*.

A Good afternoon. [1]*Could you / Do you want to* give me [2]*some / an* information about flights to Lisbon, please? [3]*I like to / I'd like to* travel on Monday morning at 8 if possible.

B Monday. OK. [4]*Let me / Can you* check.

A There aren't [5]*any / some* flights at 8, but there's [6]*an / some* earlier flight at 6:30.

B How much [7]*does that cost / is that* cost?

A 750 euros.

B That's [8]*much / a lot!* [9]*Do you have / Are you having* any cheaper flights?

A Sorry, not then. There's a flight at 15:30 on Sunday which [10]*costs / is costing* 280 euros.

B [11]*Can I / Let me* get a seat on that flight?

A Yes – but there's only one seat left! [12]*Do you want to / Do you like to* book it?

B Well, [13]*I wait / I'm waiting* to hear from my colleague.

A I [14]*would / could* hold it for you, if you like.

Vocabulary check

1 Complete the text with these words.

partners   produce   run   set up   founders

Jack Russell and Ray Fox are the [1]_____ of a film company that makes cartoon films. The two [2]_____ know each other from their student days. They decided to [3]_____ the company after making a video together at university. Now they [4]_____ a big organisation with over five hundred employees. They [5]_____ some of the best known cartoon films in the business.

2 Complete the text with the best option.

Many companies nowadays use the internet to [1]_____ goods and services to customers [2]_____ . Some companies maintain huge [3]_____ of customer information. Nowadays, different organisations collect so much [4]_____about us, it is difficult to have any [5]_____ . We need new [6]_____ to control the way we use the internet. For example, can we accept the activities of online [7]_____ who try to sell goods by sending out lots of emails that people don't want? Is it OK for companies to monitor web-browsing [8]_____ for example? When someone changes jobs, should one company pass on their personal [9]_____ to the new employer?

1	a	give	b	manufacture	c	offer
2	a	online	b	offline	c	on sale
3	a	databases	b	collections	c	stores
4	a	source	b	data	c	research
5	a	status	b	productivity	c	privacy
6	a	rules	b	rulers	c	rudeness
7	a	retailers	b	researchers	c	reporters
8	a	facts	b	customs	c	habits
9	a	records	b	reviews	c	videos

Career skills

Match the sentence halves.

1	I'm ...		a	a video production company.
2	I work ...		b	as a product manager.
3	I work for ...		c	for sales of music videos.
4	I'm responsible ...		d	a sales representative.
5	My main role is ...		e	to meet clients and sell our products.

Complete the dialogue with the questions.

Do you mean 16 per cent of all Britons?

Sorry, can you repeat the last number, please?

Sorry, did you say 16 or 60?

So that's about half?

Sorry, I didn't catch that.

Speaker   Our survey shows that about 60 per cent of Britons use the internet.

Questioner [1]_____

Speaker   60 per cent. And 48 per cent use the internet for email.

Questioner [2]_____

Speaker   48 per cent use the internet for email.

Questioner [3]_____

Speaker   Yes, that's right. About 16 per cent of people don't think the internet is useful or interesting.

Questioner [4]_____

Speaker   Yes, all Britons. About 11 per cent don't have enough money to buy a computer. But some people just dislike new technology – about 7 per cent in fact.

Questioner [5]_____

Speaker   That was 7 per cent.

Complete the dialogues with the phrases.

for all your help   meet you   Would you like to
You're welcome   Is it OK   I'm afraid
would be very nice   Can I introduce

1   A   _____ my colleague, Patrice Cherbourg?

     B   Pleased to _____ .

2   A   _____ join us at the restaurant this evening?

     B   That _____ , thank you.

3   A   Thank you so much _____ .

     B   _____ .

4   A   _____ to use this phone?

     B   I'm sorry, it isn't allowed.

5   A   _____ I can't find the details on the computer.

     B   Don't worry. I can check them later.

Unit 4
Image

www.longman-elt.com   www.economist.com

Creating a buzz

Keynotes

Image is the general **opinion** most people have of a company or product. **Brand image** is the opinion people have of a **brand**. A brand usually has a name, a **logo** (a symbol) and a design which everyone can easily recognise and which helps to **identify** it. Marketing experts work hard to create brands and **promote** the brand image through **advertising campaigns**. This process of **branding** is an important part of marketing. Most **customers** feel happier buying a **famous** brand than a product they don't know. The image of the brand has to **appeal** to the **target market**.

Brands

1 Discuss the following questions in pairs.

1 Are luxury goods expensive or cheap? Low quality or high quality?

2 *Inexpensive* and *cheap* can mean different things. What do you think the difference is?

3 Do you think goods which are *value for money* are cheap or inexpensive? Are they low quality?

2 Answer the following questions on identifying brands.

1 Look at the brands. Which group does each belong to? Luxury goods or value for money?

2 Work in pairs. Choose words or phrases to describe the image of each of the above brands.

fun	stylish	reliable	practical	fashionable	dynamic
excellent engineering		latest technology			

Speaking Is fashion important to you? What things have you got with you that you could call 'fashionable'?

Vocabulary 1 Match the words or phrases 1–5 with the meanings a–e.

1 top-end
2 haute couture
3 off-the-peg
4 fashion house
5 designer label

a clothes made in a factory, not specially for one person

b the company's name on the clothes they have designed

c a company that designs, makes and sells fashionable clothes

d the most expensive products in a range

e making and selling very expensive clothes, especially for women

1 'What is the point of top-end fashion?' Discuss this question with a partner then read the article and see what the writer says.

2 Read the article again and answer the questions.

1 Why are there only 2,000 customers for *haute couture*?
2 Do fashion houses make a profit from *haute couture*?
3 What is the main advantage of a fashion show?
4 Why is Paris the true capital of fashion? (two reasons)
5 Why is the fashion industry good for France?
6 Which city competes with France as a centre of fashion?

The Economist

Glossary

loss leader a product that is sold at a loss, but encourages people to buy more profitable products from the same company

glossy magazine a magazine using high quality paper with a lot of beautiful photos

Survey: Fashion
Fashion's favourite

The high cost of fashion shows is worth every penny to the industry

What is the point of top-end fashion? An haute couture dress can cost more than $100,000. Not surprisingly, there are no more than 2,000 haute couture customers in the world. The commercial point is that haute couture is the fashion house's loss leader. It creates the image of the brand. Someone who would never pay $20,000 for a hand-made dress might pay $1,000 for an off-the-peg dress with the same designer label—or $50 for its perfumes.

Fashion shows may be expensive, but the publicity they generate works out cheaper and more effective than spending $80,000 a page on advertisements in the glossy fashion magazines. One New York consultancy calculates that a 20-minute show, which could cost up to $500,000, generates as much publicity as $7m of advertising in American fashion magazines. Most people could never wear the clothes, but the idea is to create a buzz.

The true capital of fashion is Paris. It is home to the most famous brands, and it has the biggest number of talented designers. France's fashion and luxury-goods industry represents some 2,000 firms, 200,000 jobs and 5% of total industrial production. Include the textile industry, with 60,000 employees and the share of industrial activity rises to 8%. With advertising, graphic design and media, it all adds up to real economic weight. And France exports much of this output.

Can Paris continue to be the centre of the fashion industry? Perhaps New York, with its huge domestic market and new creative talent, will become fashion's centre in the future. But for now, the challenge for everyone is to sell: after all, fashion is a business. ∎

The
Economist

Would you pay more for a designer label? Why? / Why not?

The fashion industry

1 Choose the best definition for these words and phrases as they are used in the article.

1 hand-made   a manufactured in a factory   b made without machines

2 talented   a hard working   b having a special ability

3 firms   a companies or small businesses   b groups of workers

4 textile industry   a businesses manufacturing fabric   b businesses writing texts

5 output   a production   b shows

6 domestic market   a sales abroad   b sales in your own country

2 Complete the article with the following words and phrases.

campaigns	famous	fashion houses	shows
glossy magazines	image	publicity	wear

¹_____ , such as Versace and Yves Saint Laurent, are choosing celebrities for their advertising ²_____ . In the past, supermodels like Cindy Crawford were the main stars of fashion. Now the ³_____ are full of photos of beautiful actors such as Nicole Kidman. Louis Vuitton's latest advertisements feature the singer Jennifer Lopez, and no ⁴_____ fashion models. Newspapers are more interested in what film stars ⁵_____ to the Oscars (Academy Awards) than in fashion ⁶_____ . But people in the fashion industry still say that they cannot do without them. They create the ⁷_____ of the brand and generate a lot of ⁸_____ .

Word building

1 Complete the table with the missing words.

Noun	Adjective	Noun	Adjective
1 _____	luxurious	commerce	5 _____
fashion	2 _____	economy	6 _____
3 _____	industrial	fame	7 _____
creation	4 _____	8 _____	talented

2 How do you pronounce the words in the table? Mark the stress in each word.

luxury – luxurious

Now listen and check your answers.

Promoting the image

Dee Delaney is an independent marketing consultant. You will hear her talking about how companies communicate the image of their brand. Listen and answer the questions.

1 Companies don't just sell products. What more do they sell?
2 What three examples does Dee Delaney give of things that people buy that 'say something about who you are'?
3 What kind of men did Ray-Ban show in the photos in their advertising campaign?
4 What kind of people do their customers want to be?
5 Is Gap's StressFree clothing for men or for women?
6 What two adjectives describe the image of the brand?

Speaking

Think of examples of other famous brands. What kind of lifestyle do they sell? How do the advertisements promote the image?

Language check

Comparatives and superlatives

1 Complete the table with the examples in bold in the following sentences.

- Fashion shows are **cheaper** than advertisements.
- A show is **more effective** than advertisements.
- **The most famous** brands are in Paris.
- Off-the-peg clothes are **less expensive** than hand-made clothes.
- It is **easier** to copy than to create a new design.
- Paris has **the biggest** number of talented designers.

		Comparative	Superlative
A	Short adjectives (one syllable)	adjective + er 1_____	the + adjective + est 5_____
B	Short adjectives ending in -y (one or two syllables)	y̶ + ier 2_____	the + adjective + est
C	Longer adjectives (two or more syllables)	more / less + adjective 3_____ 4_____	the most / the least + 6_____

2 Which of the adjectives are type A and which are type C?

high   fashionable   beautiful   reliable   practical
slow   old   young

3 Write the comparative and superlative forms.

good   _____   _____
bad   _____   _____

4 Complete the sentences with *as* or *than*.

1 The British fashion industry isn't as important _____ the French or Italian.

2 Advertisements are more expensive _____ fashion shows.

3 A fashion show generates as much publicity _____ an advertising campaign.

For more information, see page 158.

Practice

1 Choose the correct words in *italics* in each sentence.

1 The US has a *bigger / more big* domestic market than France.

2 An off-the-peg dress is *more cheaper / cheaper* than an haute couture dress.

3 There aren't as many designers in London *than / as* in Paris.

4 This year's designs are *prettier / more pretty* than last year.

5 John Galliano is one of *greatest / the greatest* designers in the British fashion industry.

6 I think Stella is *most talented / more talented* than Susan.

7 Susan is *less creative / the least creative* of the group.

8 The quality of the clothes in the stores is *worse / worst* than ever before.

9 The price in France is the same *as / than* in the UK.

10 The price in the US is *lower / the lower* than in the UK.

2 Complete the text with the comparative or superlative form of the adjectives in brackets.

Giorgio Armani, founder of the Armani Group agrees that the last year has been the (¹bad) _____ for many years for fashion and luxury goods companies. When the economy is down, people don't want to spend money. Now, things are slowly getting (²good) _____ , and customers are becoming (³optimistic) _____ , but they are (⁴careful) _____ about what they buy than they were before. Quality and value for money are becoming (⁵important) _____ and it is (⁶hard) _____ for companies to sell something just because it has a designer label. People expect luxury goods to last (⁷long) _____ than other goods. Consumers are (⁸interested) _____ in fashion and design than ever before, but they expect to be able to buy the (⁹new) _____ styles for less.

Speaking

Look at the pictures of three watches. With a partner, compare them using the adjectives below. Say which one you like best and why.

heavy, light, sporty, stylish, fun, value for money, easy to read, comfortable to wear

Describing products

To sell a product successfully, you need to find a good way to describe it in product brochures, catalogues and so on. Market researchers ask consumers for their opinions because this helps them to design better products. Look at the photo of a computer desk. Match the questions 1–7 with the phrases in **bold** a–h. (Note: One question has two answers!)

1 What can you use it for?
2 Who can use it?
3 Where can you use it?
4 What special features has it got?
5 How does it look?
6 What is it made of?
7 Why do you / don't you like it?

a **It's ideal for** a small room.
b **It is /isn't designed for** use in the office or at home.
c **You can use it for** a PC or laptop.
d **It's suitable for** people of all ages.
e **It's got** lots of space for books and papers.
f It's very practical, **in my opinion**.
g **It looks** stylish.
h **It's made of** good quality wood.

Listening 3 ⊙ **1** Listen to three people giving their opinions about the desk in the picture. Do they all like it?

2 Listen again. How does each customer describe the desk? Tick the phrases that you hear in the list above

Speaking Work in pairs. You are going to describe a product to each other. Student A turn to page 137. Student B turn to page 141.

Culture at work ## Honest or diplomatic?

Your colleague is wearing a new suit and asks you what you think of it. You think it looks terrible. Do you give an honest opinion, or are you diplomatic? Some cultures believe it is important to be completely honest at all times. People respect honesty and don't feel hurt. In other cultures, people think it is better to give a false opinion than to say things that may hurt the feelings of others.

Dilemma & Decision

Dilemma: Volkswagen bugs

Brief

A few years ago, VW had two problems. 1) It was Europe's largest car manufacturer, but its best selling cars – the Golf, Jetta and Passat – were beginning to look old. VW's competitors had new models, but VW had nothing new. 2) The VW brand was based on value for money, middle-priced cars. VW customers wanted a more luxurious brand image when they got older and richer. VW didn't have any cars to offer them.

You work for VW in marketing. Consider the three options.

Idea 1   Large people carrier, seats 7–8 people
2.0 litre engine
Bigger and more luxurious than the Sharan
Price range: €25,000–€40,000

Idea 2   Top-end sports utility vehicle
Four-wheel drive, goes anywhere off-road
Heavy and powerful, with a 4.2 litre engine
Lots of electronic devices
Price range: €44,000–€78,000

Idea 3   Large, stylish executive car
6.0 litre engine
Top-of-the-range car that can compete with Mercedes and BMW
Excellent technology; fast and satisfying to drive; lots of electronic devices
Price range: €60,000–€105,000

Task 1

Work in three groups. Choose one of the following consumer groups and decide which product has the most appeal for them. Why?

Group A: Aged 50 and over, in top jobs

Group B: Aged 30–50; professionals with families; earning a lot

Group C: Younger, with a lot of money

Task 2

Form groups of three: one person from each group, A, B and C. Say what your consumer group thinks. Decide which product is best.

Write it up

Write a memo to the senior management of VW. Say which product idea you recommend for development and why.

Decision:

Listen to Ernst Jungbaum, a marketing consultant, explaining the decision that VW took.

Useful phrases

We think the ... is the best product to develop because ...

It is suitable for ...

It's ideal for ...

It looks ...

Unit 5
Success

www.longman-elt.com   www.economist.com

Passion into profit

Keynotes

A **start-up** is a new business. Many people decide to **start up** their own business because they have what they think is a good **business idea** and they want to become **entrepreneurs**. But it is important to prepare a good **business plan** before you start. You need to know if there is a **demand for** the products or services you want to offer. If you can **finance** the operation, find customers and beat the **competition**, you have a good chance of making a **profit**. Then you can call your business a **success**.

What is success?

What does success mean to you? Choose one of the following:

- a top job
- being your own boss
- earning a lot of money
- being famous
- being good at what you do
- being happy
- something else

What makes a successful company? Complete the sentences with words and phrases from the box.

demand	grow	control	market share	profit	market leader

1 A successful company has to make a _____ .
2 There has to be a _____ for your products.
3 The most successful companies _____ the market.
4 Successful companies have a bigger percentage of sales than their competitors. They have a bigger _____ .
5 A company that has the biggest sales or the best selling product in the market is the _____ .
6 Successful companies are always finding new markets and new opportunities to _____ .

1 Listen to Jake Goldrick, CEO of a medium-size technology company, explaining what makes a company successful. Check your answers to the extracts above.

2 Listen again and answer the questions.

1 What can companies do to make more profit?
2 What happens if a competitor brings out a better product?
3 What does Jake mean when he says that 'no company wants to stand still'?

Think of a successful company that you know. What makes it successful?

1 Read the article on the opposite page. Why do you think PJ Smoothies is a successful company?

2 Read the article again to find out when these things happened.

1 Harry Cragoe lived in California.
2 Harry Cragoe and Patrick Folkes founded PJ Smoothies.
3 Cragoe and Folkes imported smoothies from America from 19... to 19...
4 They started production in the UK.

3 **Read the article again and answer the following questions.**

1 Why did Cragoe think that smoothies were good?
2 Why did he decide to sell smoothies in the UK?
3 How did he finance the new business?
4 Why did he start production in the UK?
5 What is PJ Smoothies' market share?
6 Who or what are PJ Smoothies' main customers?
7 How did Cragoe lose £30,000?
8 Does Harry Cragoe think it is possible to run a business when you don't enjoy it?

Passion into profit

1 Harry Cragoe first tried a fruit *smoothie* in California in the early 1990s. He had no idea then that he was on the road to corporate success. Now he heads a multi-million-pound company — and it's all because of his passion for healthy eating.

2 'When I arrived in Los Angeles, I rented an apartment near the beach,' he remembers. 'I was very English, very white and overweight. Everyone was focused on looking good and being healthy. There were juice bars that sold drinks called smoothies and I loved them.'

3 When he returned to Britain, he found they weren't available. 'All you could find were cartons of apple or orange juice. I could see there was a real opportunity.'

4 Cragoe sold his flat, car and investments and flew back to California. He returned with a cool box packed with frozen drinks and persuaded a friend, Patrick Folkes, to help him import and sell them.

5 They founded PJ Smoothies in 1994. Initially, the firm imported frozen smoothies from America, but the business grew quickly and they didn't have the stock to meet demand. 'Up to then, we just imported the finished product,' Cragoe says. 'If a store ordered 200 bottles, we began defrosting.'

6 In 1996 Cragoe decided to set up production in Britain. He found a factory site in Nottingham, equipped it and began production. Since then, PJ Smoothies has gone from strength to strength. The company is now Britain's market leader in the fresh drinks sector, controlling just under 50% of the market. Cragoe sells more than 250,000 drinks a week in summer to big supermarkets.

7 There have been problems along the way. Cragoe lost £30,000 when his distributor went bankrupt, leaving him with hundreds of boxes of juice to distribute. But he has never lost confidence in his concept.

8 'Most of all, you've got to have fun,' he says. 'You must feel really passionate about what you're doing.'

Glossary

smoothie a mix of fruit juice and fruit purée which is thicker than normal juice

defrost make frozen goods warmer so that they are not frozen

Speaking

1 **What soft drinks are popular in your country?**

2 **Do you have an idea that you feel passionate about? Can you imagine setting up a business to sell this idea? What sort of business?**

Opposites

Find the words in the article with the opposite meaning to these words and phrases.

1 failure (paragraph 1)
2 slim (paragraph 2)
3 became smaller (paragraph 5)
4 weakness (paragraph 6)
5 earned (paragraph 7)

Business failure

Complete the text with the following words and phrases.

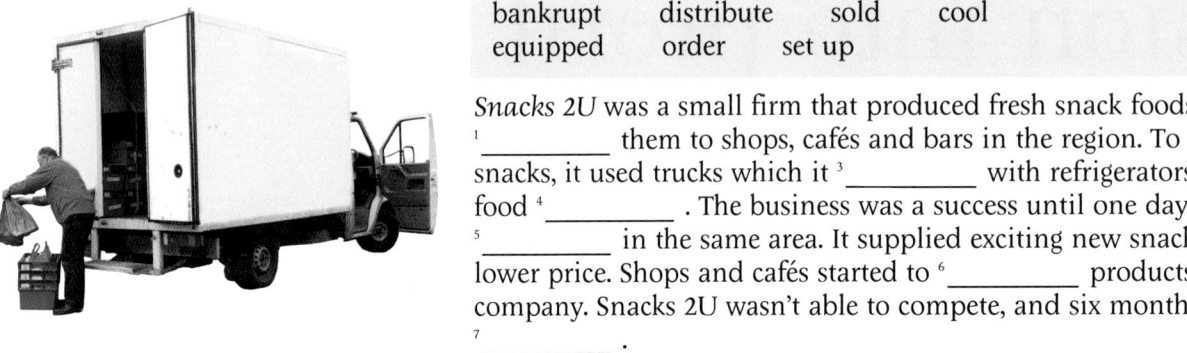

bankrupt	distribute	sold	cool
equipped	order	set up	

Snacks 2U was a small firm that produced fresh snack foods and
¹_____ them to shops, cafés and bars in the region. To ²_____ the
snacks, it used trucks which it ³_____ with refrigerators to keep the
food ⁴_____ . The business was a success until one day a new producer
⁵_____ in the same area. It supplied exciting new snack foods at a
lower price. Shops and cafés started to ⁶_____ products from the new
company. Snacks 2U wasn't able to compete, and six months later it went
⁷_____ .

Collocations

Combine words from A and B to make phrases. Use the phrases to complete the sentences below.

A	B
heads	demand
rent	fun
meet	an apartment
lose	a company
have	money

1 The person who _____ usually has the title of CEO.
2 Companies sometimes _____ when the economic situation is bad.
3 More and more people wanted to buy the new snack food. The company
   had to increase production to _____ .
4 When Patrick moved away from home to start work, he had to
   _____ .
5 Running your own business is hard work, but you can _____ too.

Setting up a new business

1 Work in small groups. Make a list of some of the things that are important to do before you start a new business.

2 Alan Martin, a young entrepreneur, describes five important steps for setting up a business. Listen and complete the chart below. Did you have the same ideas as Alan?

> Step 1: Develop _____
>
> ↓
>
> Step 2: Conduct _____
>
> ↓
>
> Step 3: Prepare a good _____
>
> ↓
>
> Step 4: Get _____
>
> ↓
>
> Step 5: Build a _____

3 Listen again and answer the questions.

1 What percentage of business ideas fail?
2 Why do they fail?
3 What two questions does your market research need to answer?
4 What two things does a business plan help you to do?
5 What does it usually include? Name three things.
6 Which step does Alan think is the most important? Why?

Speaking Alan says that most businesses fail because people don't understand the market. What other reasons for failure can you think of?

Past simple

1 Look at the examples and answer the questions.

- I **rented** an apartment near the beach.
- Harry Cragoe first **tried** a fruit smoothie in California.
- He **arrived** in Los Angeles in the early 1990s.
- When **did** Harry Cragoe **live** in California?
- **Did** they **start** production in the UK in 1992?
- They **didn't have** the stock to meet demand.

1 How is the regular past simple formed?
2 How is a question about the past formed?
3 How is the past negative formed?

2 Choose the correct words in *italics*.

The past simple describes an event that is *finished / still happening*.

3 Many verbs have an irregular past form. Look at the article on page 43 again. Find examples of irregular verbs in the past simple.

4 We often use the past simple with a time expression. Choose the correct prepositions for the time expressions below.

in	on	at	from ... to ...

1	1998	3	April 1st	5	9am
2	2003–4	4	Monday	6	March

 For more information, see page 159.

For more information, see page 159.

Writing

Read the notes about a company that makes crisps. Write complete sentences using the past simple and appropriate time expressions.

1996	→	David Willis founds Chiltern Snacks.

David Willis founded Chiltern Snacks in 1996.

1	1996–2001	→	He distributes crisps to local retailers by van.
2	August 1st 2001	→	A customer cancels his order because Willis doesn't sell 50 gram packs.
		→	Willis thinks about starting up his own brand of crisps.
3	December 2002	→	Willis starts production of the first Salty Dog crisps using 50 gram packs.
4	The first year	→	Sales grow fast.
5	November 2003	→	The first international order arrives.
6	February 14th 2004	→	Willis exports the first packs to Germany.
7	March 2004	→	He receives enquiries from the US and China.

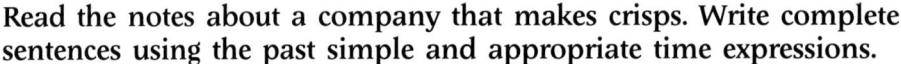

Speaking

Think of six key events in your life. Tell your partner about them and say when they happened. Ask your partner about the key events in his/her life.

Telling a story

When you tell a story in the past, it is useful to say when events happened and in what order they happened. Look at the following examples.

To begin with ...   *After about a year / after a while ...*
Then / So then ...   *After +ing ... (e.g. After graduating ...)*
For the next three or four years ...   *So what did I do?*
Two years later ...   *And now ...*

Listening 3   **1** **Listen to the story of Ben Hope. Number the events from his life in the correct order.**

lost his job   ☐   got a big contract   ☐
graduated from university ☐   employs 12 people   ☐
started his own business ☐   joined a design company ☐

2 **Listen again. Which of the above phrases do you hear?**

Speaking   **1** **Tell Ben's story in your own words. Use some of the language above.**

2 **Work with a partner. Ask and answer questions to complete the story of Jeff Bezos, who started Amazon.com. Student A read the information below. Student B turn to page 141.**

Student A

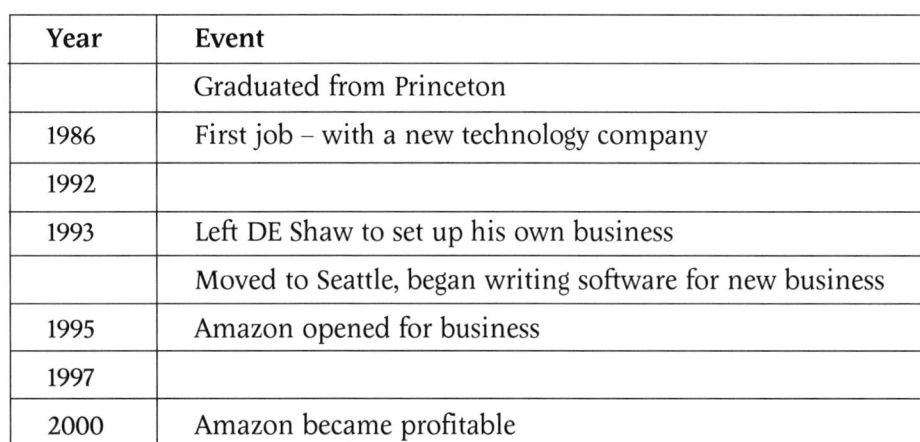

Year	Event
	Graduated from Princeton
1986	First job – with a new technology company
1992	
1993	Left DE Shaw to set up his own business
	Moved to Seattle, began writing software for new business
1995	Amazon opened for business
1997	
2000	Amazon became profitable

3 **When you have the full story, take turns to tell each part in the correct order. Use the phrases above.**

Culture at work   ## Telling stories

In some cultures, when people tell a story, they describe each event in sequence, starting with the first and finishing with the last. In other cultures, people start in the middle or at the end, and then go back to talk about earlier events. What do people do in your culture?

Dilemma &Decision

Dilemma: Organic growth

Brief

Sunshine Foods is a large dairy food producer, specialising in milk, butter, cream, yoghurt and ice cream. There is a lot of interest now in healthy food products and many consumers want to buy organic food, produced in a traditional way without the use of chemicals. Sunshine's directors want to have a share in the organic food market and they believe that the best way to enter the market is to take over (buy) a firm that already produces organic products. They plan to create a new subsidiary which, they hope, will quickly become market leader in the organic dairy food sector. Sunshine Foods is looking for an organic producer which has created a popular brand with excellent products and offers good opportunities for growth. The firm they choose should be profitable and well run, but it may need financial help to be able to grow.

Sunshine Foods is considering three organic producers with the idea of making an offer to the most suitable one. These are:

A Rocky Farm: a farm that makes its own organic ice cream.

B Annie's Kitchen: a small producer of organic ice cream and yoghurt.

C Golden Valley: a farm cooperative that produces organic milk, butter, cream and a range of different yoghurts.

Task 1

Work in three groups, A, B and C. Choose one of the above firms and read about them. Group A, turn to page 138. Group B, turn to page 142. Group C, turn to page 144.

Task 2

Prepare a short presentation about the firm. Be ready to explain:

1 the firm's history.
2 the firm's strengths and weaknesses.
3 why you think the owners may agree to a takeover.

Task 3

Make a short presentation about the firm you researched.

Task 4

After the presentations, the class should try to agree which firm Sunshine Foods should offer to buy.

Write it up

Write a memo to the directors of Sunshine Foods. Say which organic producer offers the best opportunity. Explain your reasons.

Decision:

⊙ Now listen to Ronald Dean, the CEO of Sunshine Foods, describing what decision the company took and what happened.

Unit 6
Future

www.longman-elt.com   www.economist.com

Going up?

Keynotes

Man is constantly **exploring** new possibilities and making new **discoveries**. New **technology** will shape our future and open up new **opportunities** for business. But developing a new technology takes time and needs a huge amount of **funding**. People who want to finance new **ventures** need to borrow a lot of **capital**. But it may be difficult to persuade people to **invest in** a project that is very **risky** or doesn't have the **potential** to make much profit.

Ventures into space

1 Look at the photos. What do they show? Do you know of any recent space ventures like these?

2 What are the benefits of exploring space? Are there any benefits for business?

Reading 1 **Read the description of the space elevator and answer the questions.**

1 Where will the space elevator's two platforms be?
2 What will link the two platforms?
3 How could people use the space elevator?

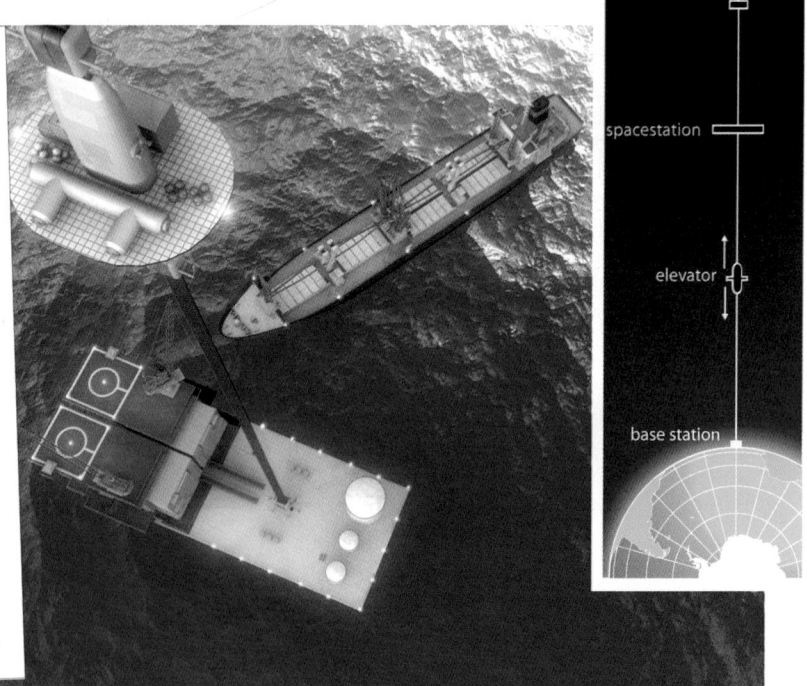

A number of scientists dream of building an elevator into space. A space elevator could link the Earth with space, and provide an easier way to send people and things up into space. To build it, you need a very strong cable which permanently connects a platform in space to a platform on the surface of the Earth. The space platform will be at the same height above the Earth as most satellites. The Earth platform will be on the sea near the equator. Astronauts and goods could travel inside a capsule which moves up and down the cable between the two platforms.

Speaking **What do you think of the space elevator idea? What benefits could it have?**

1 Read the article and find the answers to these questions.

1 What are the two main disadvantages of launching satellites into space?
2 Is the space elevator a private or a government project?
3 What two big problems does Michael Laine have to solve before he can build the space elevator?
4 What is LiftPort trying to do to solve these problems?
5 Can LiftPort make money from the space elevator? How?

2 What do these numbers refer to?

1 2018
2 $100 million
3 $7 billion to $10 billion
4 $20,000
5 5 thousand kilos

An elevator to space

Wouldn't it be nice if you could take an elevator to space?

IN the future, you may be able to. Michael Laine hopes that his new business, LiftPort Group, will complete a space elevator by 2018. But we already have rockets and satellites, so why an elevator? Well, it's not cheap to get satellites into orbit. To reach 35,793 km up – where about half of all satellites go – costs above $100 million. Add another 10% to 20% for insurance. And make sure you build that satellite right the first time because, once it's up there, you can't fix it.

The private space industry is expected to grow, but many of the new ventures like the space elevator seem extremely risky. Of course, Laine knows that things will not be easy. First of all, there's the start-up cost: He thinks that the construction of the elevator will cost between $7 billion and $10 billion over five years. Then there's the fact that the cable for the elevator needs to be stronger than anything in industrial use today – about 30 times the strength of steel.

Laine runs the company on a tight budget and employs only five people. He says he plans to raise capital and set up joint ventures with other technology businesses. When it is finally completed, the elevator could compete with NASA and the Russian Space Agency.

It wasn't so long ago that Laine himself was skeptical of the potential for making money in space. 'Other space enthusiasts were saying, "Let's go to the moon" or "Let's go to Mars,"' he remembers. 'I kept saying "What's your return on investment – your ROI?"' Currently, the cost to deliver a kilo of stuff into space using rocket launch is $20,000. The elevator could carry loads of five thousand kilos per day. It could deliver over a million kilos of material per year – resulting in billions of dollars in sales.

But with so many problems to overcome, will it ever happen?

Glossary

joint venture a business activity which two or more companies have invested in

NASA National Aeronautics and Space Administration (US space agency)

skeptical (American English) not believing what other people tell you (British English *sceptical*)

stuff objects or materials (informal)

1 Do you think the space elevator will ever happen? Why? / Why not?

2 Would you like to travel into space? Why? / Why not?

Financing ventures

1 **Match the words and phrases 1–6 with the meanings a–f.**

1	capital	a	careful control of costs, necessary when you have very little money
2	start-up cost	b	the profit you make from an activity in relation to how much money you put in
3	a tight budget	c	money you lend to someone so that they can start a business venture
4	potential	d	the time needed to get back the cost of an investment
5	return on investment	e	the expense of setting up a new business or new project
6	payback period	f	possibility of future success

2 **Now complete the text below using the words and phrases from exercise 1.**

Finance for space ventures

It is very difficult for companies in the private space industry to find the necessary [1]_____ for new space projects. Private investors don't like investing in space because the [2]_____ is high, and because the [3]_____ can be as much as 20 years or more. Investors want to be sure that they will get a good [4]_____ . However, some millionaire space enthusiasts will support projects even if there is not much [5]_____ for making a profit. Even government projects are often short of money. Most space ventures have to run on [6]_____ .

Collocations

1 **Look at the groups of words. Cross out the noun that doesn't go with the verb in each group.**

1	launch:	a satellite, a rocket, a budget, a new product
2	set up:	a satellite, a company, a joint venture, an organisation
3	raise:	money, capital, the price, a rocket
4	make:	money, a profit, an investment, a cost
5	take:	an elevator, a risk, an investment, a decision

2 **Now match these meanings with an appropriate verb and noun from exercise 1.**

To put a satellite into orbit. *launch a satellite*

1 To borrow money to finance a new venture.
2 To do something that is dangerous and could have bad results.
3 To put something new on the market for people to buy.
4 To make an agreement with another company to work together on a business activity.
5 To put money into a business activity in the hope of making a profit later.

Venture capital

1 You will hear an interview with Christoph Wiesenthal, a partner in the venture capital firm Copernica. The firm lends money to companies to help them develop products using new technology. Before you listen, discuss the questions below with a partner. What do you think his answers will be?

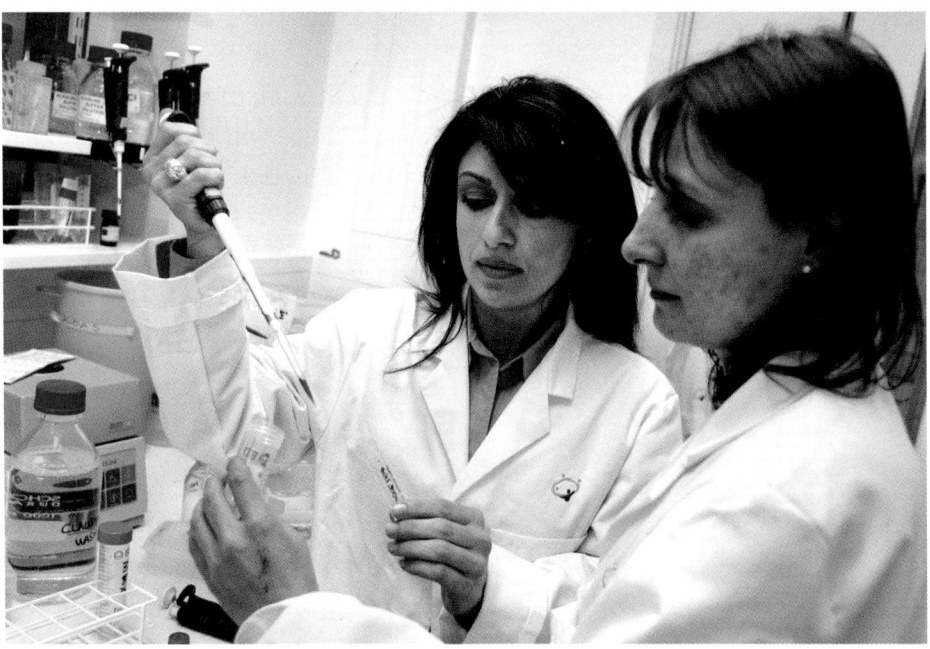

1 When you consider new projects or new ideas, what do you look for?
   a a product that will bring a return on investment in a short time
   b a product that will have a large market
2 How long do you usually have to wait to get a return on investment?
   a 1–3 years   b 5–8 years   c 12–15 years
3 What percentage of investments won't make any return?
   a 90 per cent   b 50 per cent   c 10 per cent

2 Now listen to the interview and compare your answers to Christoph Wiesenthal's.

3 Listen again and decide if the statements are true or false.

1 Copernica invests most of its capital in Information Technology.
2 Christoph Wiesenthal says it is more risky to invest in older companies than in start-ups.
3 Top scientists do not usually have a good understanding of business.

Speaking

Does Christoph Wiesenthal say anything that surprises you? Would you like to be a venture capitalist? Why? / Why not?

Modals of possibility

Look at the examples and complete the rules below.

- Michael Laine hopes that he **will** complete a space elevator by 2018.
- Things **will** not be easy.
- Laine thinks the construction **will** cost between $7 and $10 billion.
- Nine out of ten ventures **won't** make any return.
- In future, you **may** be able to take an elevator to space.
- The elevator **could** deliver one million kilos of material per year.
- Some people **might** be interested in the new product – but not many.
- They **may** not finish the construction on time.

1 We use *will/may* to make predictions that we feel certain about.
2 We usually use *will/may* after *think, hope* and *expect*.
3 We use the modal verbs _____ , _____ and _____ to make predictions that we are uncertain about and to express possibility.
4 The contraction *he'll* is the same as _____ _____ .
5 The contraction *won't* is the same as _____ _____ .

 For more information, see page 158.

Practice

1 **Make predictions. Use the positive or negative forms of *will*, *may*, *might* or *could*.**

1 In 2020, most people work from home. (certain)
2 Most meetings take place via video. (uncertain)
3 That means there is much less traffic on the road. (certain)
4 Electric cars are common. (uncertain)
5 People have more free time. (uncertain)
6 You carry your medical details on a chip under your skin. (certain)
7 There isn't enough oil to meet world demand. (uncertain)

2 **Complete the text. Use *will*, *may*, *might* or *could*.**

Ted Foster hopes that he ¹_____ be the first person to provide a private shuttle service to the moon. He's currently working on the designs and expects that the first model ²_____ be ready to fly by 2020. He has already raised $50 million, so building a prototype ³_____ (not) be a problem. But he can't be sure of raising enough money to complete the project: that ⁴_____ be much more difficult. Ted thinks the price of a ticket ⁵_____ be around $150,000 per trip. However, the price ⁶_____ be as much as $250,000 per trip. At this price, it seems that there ⁷_____ (not) be much demand for the service. Investors are worried that they ⁸_____ (not) see a big return on their investment.

Speaking

1 **Discuss the predictions in Practice 1. Do you agree with them? Change them so that they say what you think.**

2 **What major events do you think will happen in your country or region in the next year? What changes do you hope or expect to see ... in the near future? ... in five years' time? ... in the long term?**

Making predictions

People in business often have to make predictions about the future: for example, to say if they think a product or idea will be successful or not. The following phrases are useful for predicting the future. Mark each phrase certain (✓), probable (✓?), possible (??) or impossible (✗?).

- *It's possible that ...*
- *I don't think it will ...*
- *I expect it will ...*
- *I'm sure it will ...*
- *I think it's unlikely.*
- *It will probably ...*
- *This will definitely ...*
- *It may / It might / It could ...*

Listening 2 ⊙

1 A company wants to develop a new hi-tech product for the home: the Intelligent Garbage Can. It sorts your garbage, crushes it and removes the smell. Listen to four people making predictions about it. Complete column A of the table.

	A Prediction	B Phrase
John		
Jemima		
Jim		
Jo		

2 Now listen again. Which of the above phrases do they use? Complete column B.

Speaking

Which of the following products do you think you will use in the future? Make predictions using phrases from the list above.

I'll probably have a fridge that orders food from the supermarket.

Intelligent fridge: A fridge that will order food from the supermarket.

Roboservant: A robot that will do all the housework.

SafeCar: A car that doesn't need a driver.

Wristwatch computer: A computer that you wear on your arm.

Culture at work

Past or future?

Is the future more important than the past? If someone asks you what is best about your company or your country, do you talk mainly about past success, or more about future developments? Some cultures believe that past history is important because it makes us what we are today. Other cultures believe that it is better to forget the past and look forward to the future.

Dilemma & Decision

Dilemma: Risky ventures

Brief

You represent a firm of venture capitalists. You have funds to invest in an exciting new venture in a technological field. Your main interest is to see a good return on your investment with a minimum of risk.

You are going to consider three ventures, which require about $500,000 each as start-up capital:

- Celf Cure: a biotech solution for curing diseases
- Space Travel Inc.: a new spacecraft for sending tourists into space
- Fingertip: using fingerprints instead of keys to open doors

Task 1

Work in three groups, A, B and C. Each group will find out about one venture and present the details to the others. Group A turn to page 138. Group B turn to page 142. Group C turn to page 145.

Task 2

Organise your notes and prepare to present the idea to the rest of the class.

Useful phrases
The idea is …
This is how it will work …
The company wants to …
We think it will …
It has good potential because …

Task 3

Present your project idea to the rest of the class and listen to the other ideas.

Task 4

Work in different groups. Imagine you are venture capitalists and discuss which idea is the best investment.

Write it up

Write a short memo to colleagues in your company saying that you want to invest in this venture and explain why you think it will be a success.

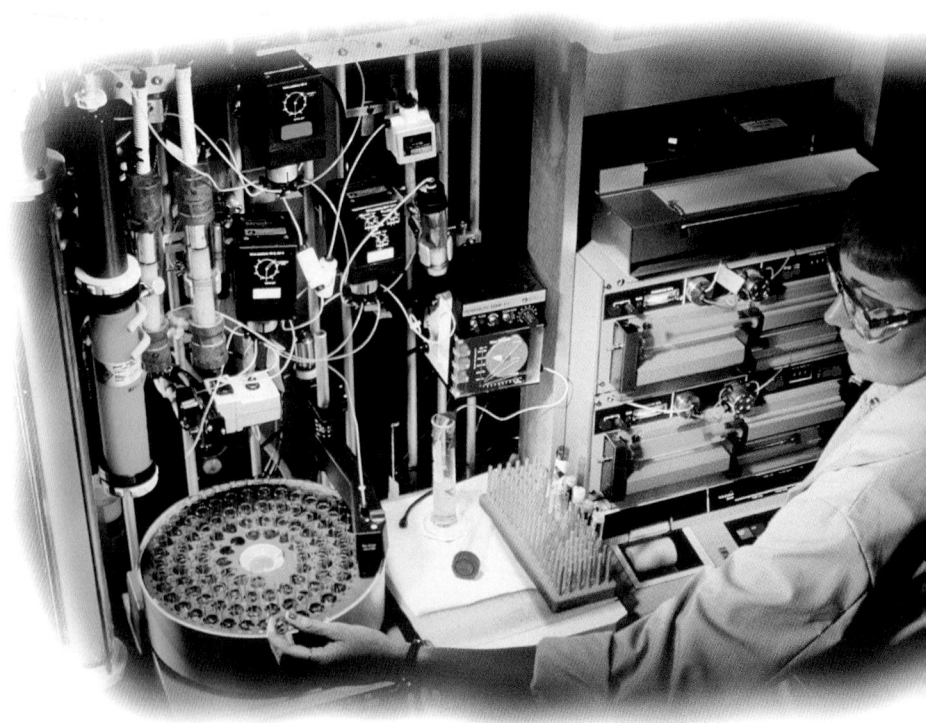

Decision:

- Listen to the venture capitalist, Christoph Wiesenthal, explaining which venture he thinks has the best potential.

Review 2

Language check

Complete the text with the correct form of the adjectives in brackets.

The hotel industry is changing. The latest trend is for (¹small) _____ , (²stylish) _____ hotels with no more than 100 rooms. These hotels are investing in (³attractive) _____ designs, (⁴comfortable) _____ furniture, and more personal service than the (⁵big) _____ hotels. Some, targeting business customers, are offering (⁶good) _____ value for money and more up-to-date technology. Among the new hotels starting up in London, the one with the (⁷low) _____ prices is the Orion, advertised at £59 per night. At the luxury end of the market, the (⁸expensive) _____ is the Seven Stars Hotel with rooms priced at £195 per night. But with no swimming pools or large function rooms to maintain, these small hotels can expect to be (⁹profitable) _____ without charging (¹⁰high) _____ than average prices.

The past simple

Complete the text with the past simple form of the verbs in brackets.

Vittorio Merloni (¹found) _____ Merloni Elettrodomestici in 1975. The company (²take) _____ just 25 years to become Europe's third-biggest maker of fridges, cookers and washing machines. It (³not start) _____ as a big company; it was a small white-goods firm which later (⁴buy) _____ the Ariston brand. Mr Merloni (⁵develop) _____ the firm by buying up his competitors and expanding his markets to other countries. He also (⁶invest) _____ a lot in research and development, and he was one of the first to use electronics in fridges and washing machines. The business (⁷grow) _____ and its sales (⁸increase) _____ reaching €2.5 billion in 2002.

Modals of possibility

Choose the correct word in *italics* to complete the sentences.

1 It's dangerous to drive when you are very tired. You *could / will* have an accident.

2 People might travel to Mars one day, but it *could / won't* be tomorrow.

3 We *may not / couldn't* have enough time to finish the work today.

4 If you're looking for a smart dress, go to Macey's. You *might / will* find what you want.

5 I'm sorry, but I *won't / may not* be able to meet you in Paris tomorrow. I'll be in London.

Consolidation

Read the text and choose the correct form of the words in *italics*.

When Kodak ¹*launch / launched* the Brownie in 1900, photography ²*become / became* a popular hobby. With the Brownie, you ³*didn't have / hadn't* to be an expert to take photos. One hundred years later, the industry ⁴*taken / took* another big step forward with the introduction of digital photography. Even the ⁵*most cheap / cheapest* digital cameras are easy to use and produce good images. So now, everyone wants one. In 2004, digital cameras ⁶*sell / sold* more than film cameras for the first time. Analysts expect that the market for digital cameras ⁷*will / is able to* double in the next year to £85 million. But an even ⁸*greater / greatest* change in the photographic industry is now taking place: mobile phones equipped with cameras are also becoming popular. In 2004, sales of camera phones ⁹*reach / reached* 190 million. This is more ¹⁰*than / as* the sales of digital cameras and film cameras together. Some analysts think that sales of camera phones ¹¹*are able to / could* reach 500 million a year in the next year or two. At present, camera phones are not as high in quality ¹²*than / as* digital cameras. But people carry their phones with them all the time, and a poor picture is ¹³*better / more good* than no picture. But ¹⁴*could / did* the technology of camera phones improve so that they start to compete with digital cameras for quality? Analysts think this is unlikely. But the quality ¹⁵*is / will* probably be good enough for most people.

Vocabulary check

Choose the correct option (a–c) to complete the text.

Pro-Chic was a ¹_____ company with a customer base of about 250. Its founder, Biruta Zilinskiene, was a ²_____ fashion designer with a lot of good ideas. She specialised in smart, practical clothes that could ³_____ to business women. Her customers were too busy to go shopping, so Biruta visited them in their office or home. It was a clever plan and Pro-Chic started to make a good ⁴_____ . The company had a brand with a good ⁵_____ , but it needed more ⁶_____ to reach a wider market. Biruta wanted the company to grow, and for that she needed to ⁷_____ her designs in magazines. To begin with, Biruta used her own money to ⁸_____ the venture. But to run a big advertising ⁹_____ , she needed a lot more ¹⁰_____ . So she went to a group of venture ¹¹_____ to try to raise more money. The group liked her ideas and saw that the business had a lot of ¹²_____ . Biruta was able to ¹³_____ the money she needed.

1	a set-up	b	starting	c	start-up
2	a talented	b	targeted	c	weak
3	a appeal	b	target	c	feature
4	a demand	b	competition	c	profit
5	a image	b	fame	c	opinion
6	a publication	b	public	c	publicity
7	a represent	b	produce	c	promote
8	a finance	b	raise	c	rocket
9	a commerce	b	contract	c	campaign
10	a findings	b	funding	c	founders
11	a capitalists	b	elevators	c	enthusiasts
12	a future	b	prediction	c	potential
13	a lend	b	borrow	c	finance

Career skills

Describing products

Match the sentence halves.

This easy to use DVD rack ...

1	... is suitable for	a	very stylish.
2	You can use it for	b	space for 100 DVDs.
3	It looks	c	strong, light metal.
4	It's got	d	busy people.
5	It's made of	e	storing all your favourite films.

Telling a story

Choose an appropriate expression to introduce each part of the story.

Then, ...   To begin with, ...   So what did he do? And now ...   For the next two years, ...   After

1 ... David worked in the clothing industry for a company called Weavers Ltd.

2 ... the company lost money and went bankrupt. Some of the managers decided to start their own business.

3 ... David worked for the new company. He saw that you could make a lot of money running your own business.

4 ... He set up his own business selling discount clothing.

5 ... six years of growth, the company had 25 stores.

6 ... David's company makes £10 million a year and employs over 2,000 people.

Making predictions

Complete each person's prediction with the most appropriate phrase.

I'll probably ...   I definitely won't ...
I think it's unlikely that I'll ...   It's possible that...
I'm sure I'll ...

1 Hector is certain he'll be a successful entrepreneur. '_____ make a lot of money.'

2 Melanie thinks she might move to a new town. '_____ stay in the same place.'

3 Simone expects to work with her father and brother. '_____work in the family business.'

4 Georg thinks he may work abroad. '_____ I'll get a job in another country.'

5 Karin is sure she will be successful in her exams. '_____ fail!'

Unit 7 Location

www.longman-elt.com   www.economist.com

Field of dreams

Keynotes

The **location** of a business can be an important **factor** for its **growth**. If a company wants to set up an office in a new location – to be near **regional markets**, for example – it needs to be sure that the **region** has good **infrastructure** and a **stable economy**. Some governments offer **low taxes** to **attract** companies to set up in **developing** regions. After deciding on the region or city for the new office, the company then has to find a good **site** for its **premises**.

A good location

Which location is best for each of the business activities 1–5? Choose from the list a–e.

1	bank	a	at an airport
2	big supermarket	b	near the sea
3	petrol station	c	in a town centre
4	duty-free shop	d	out of town
5	ship-building	e	beside a motorway

What facilities does a region need to develop as both a tourist resort and a business centre? Put the following words in the correct group.

airport apartment blocks beaches road links shopping
villas theme park port hotel

Accommodation	Infrastructure	Attractions

What else can you add to the lists?

1 Read the article on the opposite page and decide which of these statements is true.

A The future of Dubai depends on oil.
B Dubai doesn't have much potential for development.
C Dubai has a future as a tourist destination and business centre.

2 Read the article again and answer the questions.

1 What are they building on the large man-made islands off the coast of Dubai?
2 How long will Dubai's oil production continue?
3 What attractions does the city-state have for tourists?
4 What is the population of Dubai? What percentage of the people are originally from the city-state?
5 What kinds of companies are setting up business in Dubai?

3 Which of the following is complete (C), under construction (U) or planned for the future (P), at the time of writing the article?

Dubailand   Media City   Knowledge Village   Burj Dubai

Would you like to live in Dubai? Why? / Why not?

Glossary

dhow cruise pleasure trip on an Arab boat

expatriate someone who lives outside their own country

skyscraper very tall, modern city building

Dubai

Arabia's field of dreams

One of the world's most successful business ventures is a small city-state that learned lessons from Singapore and Hong Kong.

A TROPICAL sun sets behind the palm trees and white sand of Jumeirah beach. Here, machines are building houses on one of the world's largest man-made islands, designed in the shape of a palm tree (pictured). England's soccer stars, led by David Beckham, were among the early buyers when the 2,000 villas sold out in a week.

Dubai expects its oil reserves to run out in about ten years. But the city-state is using its oil income to invest in a different sort of future, replacing oil with people.

Today Dubai has 272 hotels with 30,000 rooms and almost 5 million foreign visitors a year. In the desert, Dubailand is being built—a $19-billion theme park twice the size of Disneyworld in Florida.

The city-state has built huge tax-free shopping malls and launched sporting events, such as the Desert Classic golf tournament and the Dubai World Cup horse race, and so it has become a holiday destination, offering attractions such as desert safaris and dhow cruises.

Dubai is open to foreigners. Of its 1.5 million people, over 80 per cent are expatriates. Dubai's easy-going style has made it a positive place to live and work.

In Dubai's free-trade zones, no local partner is required. These zones are attracting the service sector, by setting up developments for multi-national companies specialising in similar activities. For example, Internet City houses regional offices of Microsoft, Siemens and IBM, among others. Media City is home to the regional offices of several TV stations. There are plans for a Knowledge Village, which may attract foreign colleges.

Dubai intends to establish itself as the leading capital market for its region. The Dubai International Finance Centre is now taking shape, and the world's leading investment banks are already waiting to move in. The new city of skyscrapers includes Burj Dubai, an office block that will be the tallest building in the world when completed in a few years. Giorgio Armani is going to open a hotel on its top floors.

If it succeeds, Dubai will not only be a tourist resort but an important business centre. ∎

Collocations

1 Match the definitions 1–6 with a phrase combining a word from A and a word from B.

A	B
capital	bank
investment	company
multi-national	mall
service	market
shopping	office
regional	sector

)

1 The companies in an economy that don't manufacture anything, but provide services such as banking, insurance and tourism.

2 A company's local office in a different country or city from their main office.

3 A place where people and businesses can deal in stocks and shares, raise finance and make investments.

4 A financial institution that specialises in buying stocks and shares, and also gives financial advice to businesses.

5 A large area, often inside a huge building, where there are lots of shops.

6 A large corporation with activities in many different countries.

2 Use a collocation from exercise 1 to complete the sentences.

1 Shell is an example of a(n) _____ .

2 Hotels, restaurants and travel agents belong to the _____ .

3 Christian Hansen works as a share dealer for ABM Amros, a(n) _____ .

4 Fred Pierce is going to work abroad for two years at his company's _____ .

5 I'm going to the _____ to buy some clothes for my trip.

6 Many wealthy people invest their money in the _____ .

Multi-part verbs

Choose the correct words in *italics*.

1 The sun *set / set up* at 6:30 yesterday.

2 I'm planning to *set / set up* a new business, selling holidays abroad.

3 If you *run / run out* of money, you may have to ask the bank for a loan.

4 Many people leave their jobs to *run / run out* their own business.

5 We *sold / sold out* 50 tickets for the dhow cruise tomorrow night.

6 I wanted a ticket for the cruise, but they were *sold / sold out*.

7 The market for luxury cruises is *growing / growing up*.

8 Tom's children are *growing / growing up*. They are now 12 and 14 years old.

9 It took 20 years to *build / build up* the business to a chain of supermarkets.

10 It took six months to *build / build up* the new block for our regional offices.

What factors are important when setting up a regional office in a foreign country? Discuss the list below with a partner.

Listening ⊙ **An office abroad**

Now listen to Declan Murphy, who advises businesses on international expansion. Which of these topics does he mention?

☐ economy   ☐ access to regional markets
☐ inflation   ☐ cost of renting office space
☐ unemployment   ☐ labour costs
☐ currency   ☐ taxation
☐ prospects for growth   ☐ attitudes to foreign business
☐ infrastructure

Vocabulary 4 **Collocations**

Match the words with a topic from the list above to make a positive factor. You can use some words more than once.

a strong economy

| low | high | strong | weak | stable | easy | positive | good |

Language check **Future plans and intentions**

Study the examples and complete the rules below with the correct future form.

- Giorgio Armani **is going to** open a hotel in the Burj Dubai.
- Many of the big investment banks **are going to** set up their offices in Dubai's financial centre.
- A new train service to the city centre **is starting** next month.
- We**'re meeting** with the export manager at 3pm tomorrow.
- Thanks for your report – I**'ll read** it this afternoon.
- We**'ll try** to leave early so we can be sure to get to the airport on time.

| the present continuous | (be) going to + infinitive | will / won't |

1 We use _____ to talk about intentions when we make the decision now to do something in the future.

2 We use _____ to talk about intentions when the decision was already made before.

3 We use _____ to talk about arrangements for things to happen at a fixed time in the future.

For more information, see page 159.

1 Complete the sentences with the appropriate form of the verbs in brackets.

1 We want to build up our US sales, so we (set up) _____ a regional office in Chicago. **(intention, decision made)**

2 I (travel) _____ to Chicago tomorrow on the 8:15 flight. **(fixed arrangement)**

3 I (look at) _____ some office premises that we might rent. **(intention, decision made)**

4 How (you, travel) _____ round Chicago? **(intention)** **(two possible answers)**

5 Harry Schwarz (meet) _____ me at the airport with his car. **(fixed arrangement)**

6 We don't know which is the best location. I (collect) _____ as much information as I can. **(intention, decision made)**

7 I (present) _____ all the options after my trip. **(intention, decision now)**

2 Complete the dialogue with the appropriate form of the verbs in brackets. More than one answer is possible in some cases.

A Can you come to a meeting tomorrow at 10? We (¹discuss) _____ the plans for exporting the new model and we'd like to have your ideas.

B I'm afraid I can't. I (²leave) _____ for France this evening. I (³attend) _____ the Paris sales conference.

A When (⁴you, come back) _____ ?

B Not till next week. I (⁵stay) _____ there over the weekend.

A Well, I'm sure you'll have a wonderful time. I (⁶tell) _____ the others that you can't come.

Work with a partner. You both work in Singapore. Next Monday, some colleagues from Head Office are arriving. Discuss the plan below and decide who will do what.

What time are they arriving? Who's going to pick them up? I'll pick them up.

Plan

Monday 20th:	Colleagues arrive at the airport, 17:30
	Pick them up and take them to Palace Hotel
	Have dinner at hotel in evening
Tuesday 21st:	8:00 Meeting with sales team at the office
	10:30–13:30 Meetings with customers
	Lunch 13:30
	Afternoon: Free time to visit Singapore
	Evening: Dinner with customer at Orchid Restaurant
Wednesday 22nd:	11:00–12:30 Meeting with customer
	Lunch 12:30
	Afternoon: Short meeting on future plans
	Taxi to airport at 15:00

Write an email to your colleagues at Head Office. Explain the plan and tell them who is going to pick them up.

Making an appointment

People in business often telephone to make appointments with colleagues or business partners. The following expressions are useful.

Suggestions	Responses
I'd like to arrange an appointment.	Yes, that's fine.
Are you free next week?	I'm afraid I'm busy on Tuesday.
What about Tuesday?	I can't make Tuesday, I'm afraid.
Can we meet on Wednesday?	Wednesday is good for me.
Let's say 10 o'clock?	I'll see you at 10 o'clock then.

Put the dialogue in the correct order.

4	Can we meet on Friday then?
1	Can we meet next week to talk about the trip to Panama?
7	Yes, that's fine. See you on Friday afternoon at 3.
3	I'm afraid I can't make Thursday.
2	Good idea. What about Thursday morning?
5	Well – I'm busy on Friday morning, but I'm free in the afternoon.
6	Friday afternoon is good for me. Let's say 3 o'clock?

Speaking

Work with a partner. Prepare a plan for a trip. Complete the diary page below with the arrival and departure times. Individually, write two appointments in the diary page. Then try to arrange a third appointment with each other.

Culture at work

To plan or not to plan?

When you go on a trip or start a project, do you plan each step in advance from start to finish? Or do you wait, see what happens and make decisions later? In some cultures, people want to have a clear picture of what they are going to do. They like to make detailed plans to show how they will reach their goals. In other cultures, people prefer to react to things as they happen. This means that there is more uncertainty, but also more flexibility.

Monday
morning
afternoon
evening

Tuesday
morning
afternoon
evening

Wednesday
morning
afternoon
evening

Thursday
morning
afternoon
evening

Friday
morning
afternoon
evening

Dilemma & Decision

Dilemma: A new location

Brief

Whiterose is a group of hotels, restaurants and leisure companies which operates mainly in the UK. It is planning to expand its international operations but the head office in London is no longer big enough so the company is planning to relocate the Hotel Division.

You belong to a team that is responsible for identifying a new location for this division, which has 1,000 employees. You are looking for a town where it will be easier to find a spacious office building at a lower cost than in London. You are considering three possible towns – Luton, Swindon and Exeter.

Task 1

Decide which factors below are most important for the Whiterose Hotel Division. Can you think of any other factors?

- [ ] suitable commercial premises available
- [ ] dynamic business environment
- [ ] other companies in the same business sector in the area
- [ ] good road and rail communications
- [ ] attractive place
- [ ] close to London

Task 2

Work in three groups, A, B and C. Read about one of the three towns. Group A, turn to page 138. Group B, turn to page 142. Group C, turn to page 145.

Group A, turn to page 138. Group B, turn to page 142. Group C, turn to page 145.

Task 3

Tell the other groups about the town you researched.

Task 4

Hold a meeting to decide which town offers the best location for the new offices of the Hotel Division.

Write it up

Write a memo to the staff of the Hotel Division. Begin as follows:

To the staff of the Hotel Division

As you already know, the Whiterose Head Office can no longer provide enough space for all our employees. We are therefore planning to relocate the staff of the Hotel Division to new offices in _____ .
We believe that this will be an excellent location for you because ...

Decision:

○ Now listen to Charles Jerome who owns a commercial property agency and gives advice to businesses that are relocating their offices. He is going to explain the decision that Whiterose took.

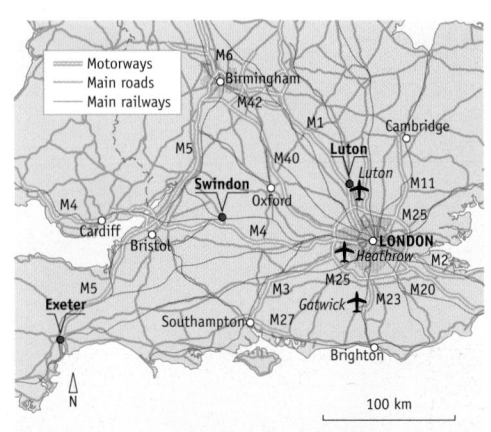

Unit 8
Job-seeking

www.longman-elt.com   www.economist.com

A monster success

Keynotes

Job-seekers look for work in the **job market**; employers offer jobs to people with the right **qualifications** and **experience**. People who know what kind of job they want can look at **job advertisements** for a suitable **position**. Others may go to **careers advisers** to ask for help in starting or managing their careers. Large companies have a **Human Resources** Department, which deals with **recruitment** and **hiring** employees, and also manages **career development** within the company.

Starting a career

What ways do you know of finding a job? Work with a partner and make a list.

Look at newspaper advertisements.

Match the words and phrases 1–3 with the definitions a–c.

1   apprenticeship

2   work placement

3   graduate trainee scheme

a   Students often take a temporary job during their studies – for little or no pay – because they want to get experience.

b   Big companies accept a number of newly qualified people to work for one year. They get general experience by working in different departments. They may or may not get a permanent job at the end.

c   A young person learns a skill or trade by working under supervision in a company. They have a contract to work there for a fixed number of years.

How do people usually start their careers in your country?

 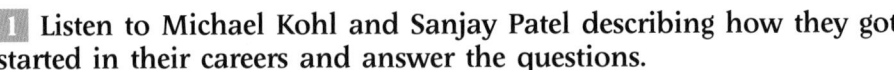

1 Listen to Michael Kohl and Sanjay Patel describing how they got started in their careers and answer the questions.

1   What reason does Michael give for choosing the company where he works?

2   How did Sanjay find a work placement?

2 Listen to Michael again and answer the questions.

1   What is Michael's job now?

2   How many applicants did VW accept on the apprenticeship scheme?

3   Michael got a qualification in what subject?

3 Listen to Sanjay again and answer the questions.

1   What subject did Sanjay study?

2   When did Sanjay do his work placement at Meridian?

3   What is his job now?

---

1 Read the article on the opposite page and find information about the following.

1   the Monster.com name

2   the image of Monster.com

3   Monster.com's biggest contribution to the recruitment industry

4   headhunting firms

---

2 **Read the text again and answer the questions.**

1 Does Monster.com make a profit?
2 What two advantages does Monster.com offer to job-seekers?
3 Find two advantages for employers of using the Monster.com site.
4 Which two kinds of business are losing money because of Monster.com's success?
5 What advice does the article give to people who want to use the site to find a job?

The Economist

Glossary

ad advertisement

resumé (American English) summary of your education and previous jobs, which you use when you are looking for a job British English: *CV* (Curriculum Vitae)

filter software that selects the job-seeker's details to match the employer's requirements

headhunting persuading someone to leave their job and go to work for another company in a similar position

Face value

The online job market

How Jeff Taylor changed the way the labour market works

Monster.com, the world's biggest online job-search site, shows how electronic marketplaces reach more people and can offer more efficiency than physical markets. It also shows that money can be made in such markets: Monster has a long record of profitability.

Jeff Taylor, who launched the site in 1994, says that the Monster.com name is the firm's "single most important success factor". It introduces an image of youthful fun in what is basically a boring business. Supporting the brand is a big advertising budget which accounts for a quarter of the firm's costs. He runs expensive ads during key sporting events such as the Super Bowl.

Job-seekers supply resumés and employers pay to scan them or to post job ads. Most of the services that job-seekers get are free, but they have to pay for a service that allows them to contact each other for advice and career management. They can use this service to ask each other questions about, say, what it is like to work for a firm that they are thinking of joining.

The main contribution of Monster has been to speed up hiring and vastly increase the accuracy of the job-search process. "You can post a job at 2pm and get your first response at 2:01," Mr Taylor says proudly. And an employer who knows exactly what he wants can use Monster's filters to search vast numbers of resumés with precise accuracy. Monster is a serious threat to newspapers, which historically made 40% of their revenues from carrying ads, up to half of which were for staff. Headhunting firms have also lost business, because demand for their help in filling lower-level jobs has fallen.

The online job market works well for workers and employers who know what they want. It works badly for people who are unsure. Check that your resumé says clearly what kind of job you want. The filters will then make sure that it reaches the right human resource departments. ∎

The Economist

Speaking **Would you use an online job-search site like Monster to look for a job? Why? / Why not?**

Vocabulary 2 Activities

Who does each of the following activities? Write E for employer and J for job-seeker.

search job ads	post a job ad	hire
scan resumés	supply resumés	fill jobs
recruit staff	use career management service	join a firm

Vocabulary 3 The application process

Complete the diagram with the following words.

accepts attend apply advertisement
candidates invites offers

1 Employer posts a job __________ on a website or in a newspaper

2 Job-seekers __________ for the post

3 The employer selects suitable __________

4 The employer __________ the selected candidates for interview

5 Candidates __________ their interview

6 The employer __________ the job to the best candidate

7 The candidate __________ or declines the offer

Vocabulary 4 Finding a job

Complete the text with the following words and phrases.

accept applications interview job ads recruit
selected resumé offered

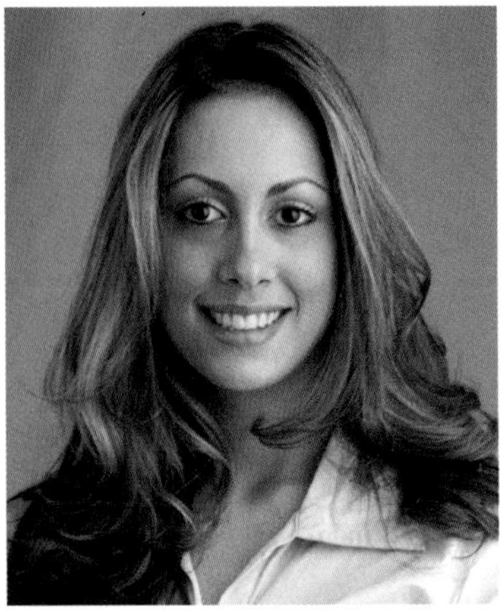

Esther Garcia graduated from university with a degree in telecommunications. But finding her first job was very hard. She searched all the [1]__________ in the newspapers and on the internet. She made lots of [2]__________ to different companies. She also sent her [3]__________ to all the big telecommunications companies. But most companies didn't even invite her for [4]__________ . It seemed that they only wanted to [5]__________ people with job experience. After several months, a finance company in Madrid [6]__________ Esther a place on a three-month graduate trainee scheme. At the end of the three months, Esther was the only person out of the ten trainees to be [7]__________ for a permanent job. Of course, Esther was very happy to [8]__________ .

1 Read the ad from the Monster.com site. Would this job be good for someone who ...

1 ... wants to live in New York?

2 ... wants a part-time job?

3 ... is looking for their first job?

4 ... has experience in office administration but not in Human Resources?

5 ... doesn't have any specific Human Resources qualification?

6 ... has a university qualification?

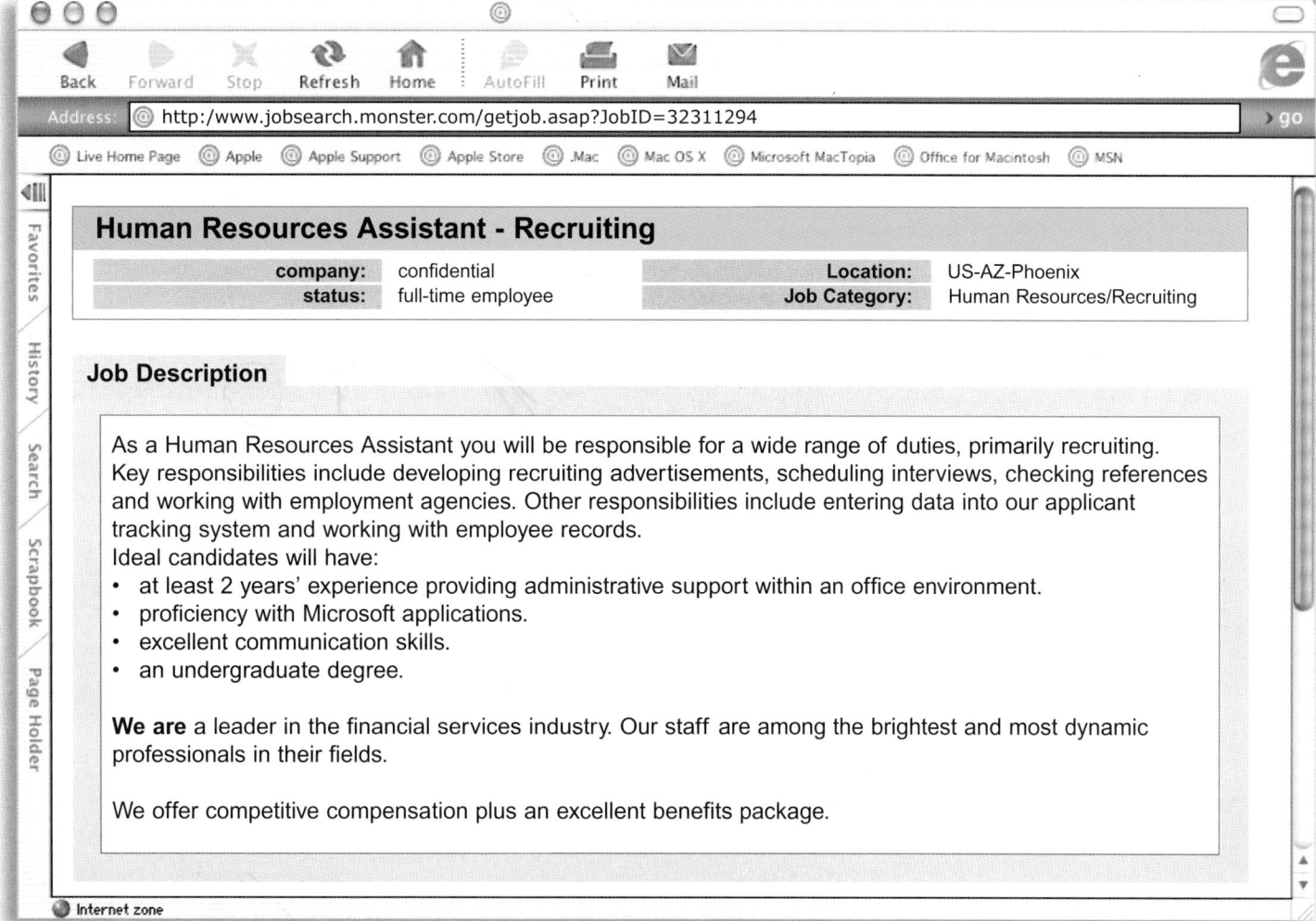

Human Resources Assistant - Recruiting

| **company:** | confidential | **Location:** | US-AZ-Phoenix |
| **status:** | full-time employee | **Job Category:** | Human Resources/Recruiting |

Job Description

As a Human Resources Assistant you will be responsible for a wide range of duties, primarily recruiting. Key responsibilities include developing recruiting advertisements, scheduling interviews, checking references and working with employment agencies. Other responsibilities include entering data into our applicant tracking system and working with employee records.

Ideal candidates will have:

• at least 2 years' experience providing administrative support within an office environment.
• proficiency with Microsoft applications.
• excellent communication skills.
• an undergraduate degree.

We are a leader in the financial services industry. Our staff are among the brightest and most dynamic professionals in their fields.

We offer competitive compensation plus an excellent benefits package.

2 Find a word or phrase in the ad which means:

1 most suitable applicants

2 a minimum of

3 a high level of ability or skill

4 ability to express yourself clearly and understand the needs of others

5 salary

6 something you get in addition to salary (e.g. health insurance, pension scheme)

Speaking **What would be interesting or not interesting about this job, in your opinion?**

The imperative

Match the examples of the imperative 1–5 with the uses a–e.

1 **Check** that your resumé is clear.
2 **Pass** me that book, please.
3 **Don't touch!**
4 **Let's take** a break.
5 **If you aren't** sure, **ask** for help.

a   a polite instruction
b   an instruction not to do something
c   a conditional instruction
d   advice
e   an informal suggestion

 For more information, see page 159.

Practice

1 Complete the sentences with *Let's*, *Don't* or *Please*.

1 This equipment is very expensive. _____ be careful with it!
2 I don't want anyone to know about my new job yet. _____ tell anyone.
3 It's one o'clock. _____ go for lunch.
4 It's good to try different kinds of work. _____ be afraid to change jobs.
5 It's a good job and we're offering you a very good salary. _____ think about it.
6 We don't have time to discuss this question now. _____ leave it till tomorrow.
7 _____ turn off all the lights when you leave the office.

2 Complete the instructions with the correct form of the verbs in brackets.

1 If the machine breaks down, (phone) _____ the maintenance department.
2 If you (not understand) _____ a word, look it up in a dictionary.
3 Please (tell) _____ your head of department if you want to attend the seminar.
4 Please (not enter) _____ the room if the red light is showing.
5 If you can't find the room, (ask) _____ at reception.
6 If you (be) _____ tired, let's take a break.

Speaking

Work with a partner. Choose one of the following situations and prepare six 'dos and don'ts' to help someone. Report your list to the rest of the class.

– Finding the right university or college   *Search the internet …*
– Finding the right course or training programme
– Choosing a good company to work for

Explaining what to do

When you start a new job, your new colleagues may have to explain a lot of things to you in the first few weeks. When you have more experience, you may need to give explanations to other new staff. The following phrases are useful for explaining how to do something. Which ones express important instructions and which are just suggestions?

1 *Make sure that ...*

2 *It's important / essential that ...*

3 *Remember to ...*

4 *Don't forget to ...*

5 *It's a good idea to ...*

6 *It may be better / best to ...*

Preparing a CV

1 Listen to Barry Hampton, a careers adviser, explaining how to prepare a CV for a UK job. Which of the following points does he advise? Tick the points that are correct, and change the points that are not correct.

1 Write more than two pages.

2 Start with details of previous jobs.

3 Leave out your date of birth.

4 Don't say anything about hobbies and interests.

5 Give the contact details of two references at the end.

2 Listen again. Which of the above phrases does he use?

1 Practise giving advice for preparing a CV for a UK job. Use the list in Listening above, including your corrections, and choose phrases from above to introduce each point.

2 Work with a partner. Practise explaining one of the following to a British person.

– Where to look for a job in your country.

– How to prepare a CV for a job in your country.

– What to wear for an interview.

Fixed procedures or flexibility?

When you are part of an organisation or a team, do you think it is best to have a fixed way of doing things that is made clear to everyone? Or is it better to be flexible? In some cultures, people like to have specific rules and procedures to follow. In other cultures, people prefer to have flexible ways of working. They prefer to deal with each situation separately in the way they think is best.

Dilemma & Decision

Dilemma: For love or money?

Brief

Kate Gray is in a happy position: she has two job offers. The problem is to choose the job that will suit her best. Kate is a new graduate in geography and wants to work in the travel industry. She would like a job that includes travelling and working with people. Two different travel companies are offering her a position. She has the chance to work in the marketing department of Wide World Tours, a big company with 3,000 employees and regional offices around the world. Or she could work for Oz Travel, a small company which has only 19 employees and specialises in tours to Australia. You work for a career advisory service. Kate asks you to help her make the correct choice.

Task 1

Work in three groups. Find out more information about Kate's situation.

Group A: Research the job with Wide World Tours. Turn to page 138.

Group B: Research the job with Oz Travel. Turn to page 142.

Group C: Find out more about Kate's personality and preferences. Turn to page 145.

Task 2

Form new groups: Your group should include at least one person from A, B and C above. Make a list of the advantages and disadvantages of each job offer. Then match the advantages of each job with Kate's preferences, personality and ambitions. Decide which job will suit her best.

Think about these topics:
1 Role and responsibilities
2 The company
3 Pay
4 Career prospects

Write it up

Write an informal letter to Kate. Give her some advice based on your discussion in Task 2.

Useful phrases
It's a good idea to …
It's important to …
It may be better / best to …

Decision:

⊙ Listen to Barbara Kingsland, a careers adviser, explaining what advice she would give to Kate. Then listen to Kate saying what decision she made and what happened.

Unit 9
Selling

www.longman-elt.com   www.economist.com

Hard to reach

Keynotes

Many manufacturers sell their products through retailers, but they may also sell **direct** to the **consumer** by telephone or on the internet, or they may employ **sales representatives.** A lot of companies sell products and services business to business, or **B2B.** Product information is created in the form of **flyers** or **catalogues** and some companies send this information to large numbers of **potential customers** through the post. This **method of selling** is called **direct mail. Marketers** are always looking for ways to **promote** their products to new kinds of customer.

Promoting the product

Companies use a number of different methods to promote and sell their products or services. Study the notes and discuss in pairs how to complete them.

> **Methods of selling**
>
> 1 Advertising media: TV, _____
>
> 2 Personal selling: employing _____
>
> 3 Sales promotions: special offers, _____
>
> 4 Public relations: creating _____
>
> 5 Direct marketing: direct mail, _____
>
> 6 Sponsorship: where a company pays to have its name linked to an _____
>
> or a _____

Listening 1 ⊙ Now listen to Mario Capelli, a marketing consultant, describing different methods of promotion. Complete the notes above.

Reading **1** Read the article on the opposite page and answer the questions.

1 How much money do UK students spend in a year in total?

2 Find two reasons why it is difficult to sell products to students.

3 How does *The Guardian* help students?

4 What are 'energy teams'?

5 Why is it important to use students and not company sales reps to sell products?

6 How can marketers learn more about student life?

2 Match the companies 1–4 with the promotion method they use a–e, as described in the article. One company uses two methods.

1	Carling	a	offers discounts on products
2	*The Guardian*	b	employs students to sell on campus
3	Red Bull	c	asks students to help plan special events
4	Virgin D3	d	organises music events in public places
		e	offers help with education and careers

MARKETING TO STUDENTS

The student market in the UK is estimated to be worth £13 billion of spending power in a year. It is a market no company should ignore. Marketers are desperate to get students' attention before they turn into high-earning graduates. But students are hard to reach and cynical. How can brands target them?

Youth market trends analyst Sean Pillot de Chenecey advises companies who hope to market to students. He says there is no single strategy. Students organise their life on their mobile phones, respect brands that are ethical, but worry more about how they're going to pay off their debt than world peace. To get students' attention, marketers must offer them something that adds to their lives. It isn't enough to simply sponsor a music tour: they have to make the event happen. For example, Carling (a beer manufacturer) introduced live music on the Tube.

Offering students help with their education and careers is an effective marketing method. *The Guardian* newspaper runs careers fairs and offers discounts on its products, such as *Guardian Student*, a 32-page newspaper.

Red Bull, a successful energy drinks brand, uses what it calls 'energy teams' on university campuses. The company recruits teams of students and gives them a Red Bull car, which has a fridge. The students offer samples and give information about the product benefits.

They do this on campus at sporting events and at times of the year when students might need an energy boost. 'It's extremely important that it's a student doing this and not a company sales rep,' says the company's consumer manager who runs the scheme. 'You need to have an approach that doesn't look like a sales pitch.'

Having an insider on campus can help marketers understand student life. Youth marketing agency, Virgin D3, has a database of students who act as 'field staff'. They ask them for help when planning an event at their university. Perhaps, by getting ideas from the students themselves, companies can find ways to reach this difficult market.

Glossary

cynical not believing that people are sincere or honest

the Tube London's underground train system (informal)

sales rep sales representative (informal)

sales pitch selling something by saying how good it is

insider someone who is part of an organisation and so has special knowledge of it

---

Speaking

1 'Students have a strong sense of social responsibility and ethical branding. They want companies to behave well.' What do you think of this description of UK students? Could you describe students in your country in the same way?

2 What ethical reasons could people have for not buying from a particular company? Are there any companies whose products or services you would never buy?

Complete the sentences with these words and phrases from the article.

> boost   debt   discount   estimate   high-earning
> method   pay off   spending power   worth

1   The market for new cars is _____ about €200 million a year.

2   We _____ that our share of the market will be 28 per cent.

3   We are targeting _____ consumers with salaries above €100,000 a year, who have enormous _____ .

4   Many of our customers have a _____ of €5,000 or more.

5   It will take them several years to _____ these loans.

6   We have a special offer this month: a 5 per cent _____ on all software products.

7   We are trying a new _____ of selling: sending special offers by text message.

8   The company hopes that its new strategy will give sales a _____ .

Word building

1 Complete the table.

Noun	Person	Verb
1 _____	2 _____	sponsor
consumption	3 _____	4 _____
marketing	5 _____	6 _____
7 _____	8 _____	organise
analysis	9 _____	10 _____
11 _____	agent	no verb

2 Change the form of the words in *italics* in the text.

Make espresso coffee at home

With an exciting new machine, you can now make the perfect espresso coffee at home. Nestlé Nespresso, part of the Nestlé Group, has combined an excellent product design with clever [1]*market* to completely change coffee [2]*consume* at home. A recent [3]*analyse* of the espresso market, carried out by the market research [4]*agent* Adpro, shows that the potential for sales of Nespresso machines is huge. For example, 70 per cent of the French [5]*consumer* espresso, but only 10 per cent have a machine at home. Nespresso sells coffee capsules for its machines through the Nespresso Club, which allows [6]*consumption* to order online. The company is a [7]*sponsorship* of the sailing team, Alinghi, in its campaign to win the Americas Cup. This [8]*sponsor* deal is a perfect match between two dynamic world teams.

A product launch

1 How can companies attract attention when they launch a new product?

2 Toshiba Network Products (TNP) sells components to cable TV and internet companies. Listen to their communications manager, Michio Yano, explaining how they launched a wireless modem in the US. Choose the best option to complete each sentence.

1 TNP launched the modem a at a trade fair b with a big party c at a customer's offices.
2 They contacted customers a by mail b by email c by email and phone.
3 They sent a total of a two b three c four mailings.
4 At the launch, customers could watch demonstrations of the product on TV and a have fun b eat lunch c read product brochures.
5 The number of people who attended was a 250 b 500 c 600.

Speaking **1** Was the TNP launch successful? Why? / Why not?

2 What are the advantages and disadvantages of using email to contact customers?

Language check **Modals of obligation**

Study the examples and complete the table with the words in bold.

- Companies **have to** follow certain rules when advertising their products.
- For example, they **mustn't** give false information in their advertisements.
- Marketers **must** offer students something that adds to their lives.
- You **need to** have an approach that doesn't look like a sales pitch.
- Marketers **shouldn't** ignore the student market.
- You **should** find out what appeals to your target market.
- You **don't have to** have sales experience to join a team.
- You **don't need to** send sales reps to student events.

It's the rule	1 _____ or	It isn't allowed	5 _____
This is strong advice	2 _____	Strong advice not to	
Advice or recommendation	3 _____	Advice or recommendation not to	6 _____
It is necessary	4 _____	It isn't necessary	7 _____ or 8 _____

must or *have to?* We usually use *must* when we make the rule ourselves, and *have to* when it is a general rule. So *must* and *mustn't* can seem impolite. Use *have to* or *shouldn't* when talking to people you don't know well.

⤵ For more information, see page 158.

1 As a special promotion, *Camera Eye*, a photographic magazine, is running a competition to win a digital camera. Complete the rules using *must, must not, don't have to, need to, don't need to*.

★1 Employees of *Camera Eye* _____ enter the competition. (it isn't allowed)

★2 All entries _____ arrive by December 31st. (it's the rule)

★3 You _____ be a regular subscriber to *Camera Eye*. (it isn't necessary)

★4 You _____ enclose a self-addressed envelope with your entry. (it is necessary)

★5 You _____ enter more than three photos. (it isn't allowed)

★6 You _____ send all your entries at the same time. (it isn't necessary)

★7 You _____ write your name and address on the back of each photo. (it's the rule)

★8 You _____ accept the decision of the judges as final. (it's the rule)

2 Rewrite a sales trainer's advice to shop assistants on a training course using *must, mustn't, should, shouldn't*.

It's important not to talk too much: many customers don't like it.

You mustn't talk too much.

1 It's essential to know as much as possible about the products.
2 Don't be afraid to start a conversation with the customer.
3 It's better not to start with a sales pitch straightaway.
4 I recommend that you ask a few questions to find out your customer's needs.
5 Make the customer feel comfortable and important.
6 It's a good idea to suggest different products that the customer could be interested in.
7 I strongly advise you to stress the benefits of the product, not the features.
8 It's important not to spend too long with one customer when others are waiting.

Speaking   How important are the qualities below for a sales representative? Which ones are essential, which are quite important and which are not necessary? Discuss them with a partner using *must, have to, should, shouldn't, doesn't have to*.

☐ enthusiastic   ☐ good communication skills
☐ outgoing   ☐ punctual
☐ fashionable   ☐ creative
☐ relaxed   ☐ expert
☐ energetic

Making suggestions

When you are part of a team, for example a sales team, it is important to contribute ideas. The team may hold meetings where you have the chance to make suggestions. Study the expressions below for making suggestions and responding. Which responses mean *yes* and which mean *no*?

1	*How about / What about + -ing?*	a	*That's a good idea.*
2	*Why not ... ?*	b	*I'm not sure about that.*
3	*I think we should ...*	c	*That could be difficult.*
4	*We need to ...*	d	*I like that!*
5	*Perhaps we could ... ?*	e	*Brilliant!*

Listening 3 ⊙

1 Cookwell has a chain of stores selling top quality kitchen equipment. The sales department decides to offer cooking classes as a way to increase business. Listen to members of the sales team suggesting ways to promote the cooking classes. Does each suggestion receive a positive or negative response? Mark the suggestions with a tick (✓) or a cross (✗).

Suggestion	✓/✗	Suggestion phrase (1–5)	Response phrase (a–e)
1 Put up posters.			
2 Hand out leaflets to customers.			
3 Put details on the website.			
4 Collect customers' contact details and mail them directly.			
5 Invite someone from the press.			

2 Listen again. Which phrases above are used for suggesting and responding? Write 1–5 and a–e in the table.

Speaking

Work in small groups. You work in the sales department of a chain of hairdressing salons. How can you promote your salons to young people? Make suggestions.

Culture at work

Showing reactions

When a business partner or colleague suggests an idea to you, do you immediately show what you think or not? In some cultures, people show strong reactions to other people's ideas, for example, 'That's brilliant!' or 'That's crazy!' In other cultures, people are more careful about their response, and it is not easy to tell what they are really thinking. What are people like in your culture?

Dilemma & Decision

Dilemma: Guerrilla marketing

Brief

Virgin Mobile is a phone operator that provides a wide range of mobile communication services to its customers in the UK. Competition between mobile phone operators is strong and winning a large market share in the student market is vital. Students use their mobile phones a lot – to call friends and family, and also to get information and play games. There are 2.5 million students in the UK, and 96 per cent of them own a mobile phone. But it is difficult to market to students because they are hard to reach and are cynical about sales pitch. Virgin Mobile has decided that the best way to promote the brand to students is to find insiders: student marketers who will work on promotional campaigns in their own universities.

The problem for Virgin Mobile is how to identify student marketers with brilliant ideas and good selling skills. There are three options:

1 Use standard job recruitment methods.
2 Recruit people at student fairs.
3 Hold a competition.

Task 1

Work in groups. You are marketing consultants. Read about one of the options then discuss how it might work. Group A turn to page 139. Group B turn to page 143. Group C turn to page 145.

Task 2

Form new groups: your group should include at least one person from A, B and C above. Present your ideas to your group.

Task 3

Discuss the three options and for each one decide if you think it could work or not. If not, why not? Then decide on the option which you think will be most effective in identifying talented student marketers. You could decide on a combination of two options.

Write it up

Write an email to Virgin Mobile. Tell them which option you think will be most effective. Explain your decision and how you think it could work.

Decision:

Now listen to Nikki Lambert from the Virgin Mobile brand marketing department talking about the methods that the company used to identify student marketers.

Useful phrases

I / We think it's best to …
We need to …
That's a good strategy because …
It could be difficult because …
Perhaps we could …

Review 3

Language check

Future plans and intentions

Complete the dialogue with the appropriate form of the verbs in brackets: *going to*, *will* or the present continuous.

A Hi, Richard. I'm afraid I've got some bad news. I ('not come) _____ to Bahrain tomorrow.

B But we (²meet) _____ Ahmed on Wednesday to discuss the sales figures!

A I know. I'm sorry but we've got problems with the launch of the G42. I've decided I (³stay) _____ at head office to put things right.

B (⁴you, come) _____ next week instead?

A I don't know yet. I (⁵phone) _____ you on Friday. We (⁶talk) _____ about it then.

B OK. But you know Ahmed (⁷travel) _____ to Singapore the week after, so he (⁸not be) _____ free to meet with us then.

The imperative

Find and correct the mistake in each sentence.

1 Let's to discuss the new trainee scheme next.

2 If the company will offer you a job, accept it!

3 Please not to touch the equipment!

4 Please to be careful to use the right form.

5 You don't use this phone – use that one.

6 If Jo phones, please you will take a message.

7 If you will not have the right qualifications, don't apply for the job.

8 Please you tell me if you can't hear.

Modals of obligation

Match the underlined phrases with a modal verb phrase a–h that has the same meaning.

1	It's essential to pay off your debts on time.	a you shouldn't
2	It isn't allowed to use a mobile phone in here.	b you don't have to
3	It isn't necessary to be a graduate to apply for this job.	c you don't need to
4	The rule is: show your passport when you buy foreign currency.	d you should
5	My advice is: search the web if you want to find a good job.	e you mustn't
6	It isn't necessary to pay now, you can pay next week.	f you need to
7	My advice is: don't go to a job interview without good preparation.	g you must
8	It's necessary to have sales experience if you want to join the team.	h you have to

Consolidation

Choose the correct words in *italics*.

Good morning everybody and welcome. All of you have chosen to join the international division. So that means that ¹*you started / you're going to start* a new job in one of our regional offices. At 10 o'clock, Delores Tavares ²*will come / is coming* to talk to you about culture. But first ³*I'm explaining/ I'm going to explain* a few points to help you prepare for the move to a new country. Please stop me if you ⁴*will have / have* any questions. First, some practical points. You ⁵*will / must* make sure that your passport is up-to-date. And if you need to apply for a visa, ⁶*please do it / let's do it* as soon as possible. It can take a lot of time, so ⁷*you don't have to / you mustn't* leave it till the last minute. The administrative staff will help you. Some of you ⁸*travel / are travelling* with your families so you'll ⁹*have to / should* check the travel documents for your family.

Now each of you ¹⁰*is having / is going to have* a one-week trip to your new location before you start the job. This trip ¹¹*will give / is giving* you the chance to find out about the new environment. ¹²You *need / should* make the best use of this trip. We want you to start your new job without too many problems. As you know, you ¹³*mustn't / don't have to* look for accommodation because the company is going to provide you with an apartment. But ¹⁴*don't / you don't* expect everything to be easy. The way of life in other countries is often very different. You ¹⁵*shouldn't / don't have to* forget that!

Vocabulary check

1 Choose the correct option a–c to complete the text.

Buenos Aires is a leading business ¹_____ . It has a ²_____ economy. International trade plays a key role in the ³_____ of the city. The country exports many products through its historic ⁴_____ . Many international banks have their ⁵_____ offices here.

1 a location   b site   c placement
2 a large   b strong   c fat
3 a growing   b development   c increase
4 a airport   b pitch   c port
5 a regional   b capital   c investment

2 Choose the correct option a–c to complete the text.

What ¹_____ do you need to work in sales? Nicholas, 33, a sales director with a food producer, says: 'You don't need a university ²_____ , but it helps. It's more important to be energetic and ³_____ – able to talk easily to all kinds of people. You also need good management ⁴_____ . If you really want to develop your ⁵_____ , you can earn a good ⁶_____ .'

1 a quality   b qualifications   c values
2 a graduate   b benefit   c degree
3 a outgoing   b communicating   c respectful
4 a skills   b specialities   c statistics
5 a currency   b compensation   c career
6 a payment   b salary   c potential

Career skills

Making an appointment

Complete the dialogue with the following words and phrases.

free   I can't make   see you   Let's say
I'm afraid not   Can we meet   I'd like to arrange

A I'm going to be in Riga next week and ¹_____ a meeting with you and Jurga, if that's possible.

B OK. It would be good to meet you while you're here. ²_____ on Friday?

A ³_____ . I'm only in Riga from Monday to Thursday. But I'm ⁴_____ on Tuesday and Wednesday. What about you?

B ⁵_____ Wednesday morning, but the afternoon is good for both of us. Can you come to the office? ⁶_____ at 2 o'clock?

A Yes, that's fine. I'll ⁷_____ on Wednesday at 2 o'clock, then.

Explaining what to do

Choose the correct words in *italics*.

1 You don't have to stay in a job that you don't like: it may *make sure / be better* to look for a new job.

2 But first, it's *important / sure* to decide what you really want to do.

3 It's *a good / a best* idea to make a list of your strengths, skills and interests.

4 And don't *remember to / forget to* add a list of what you like and dislike about your present job.

5 Then make *sure / essential* that you look for opportunities that match your abilities and interests.

Making suggestions

Complete the dialogue with the following words and phrases.

we could   why   I think we should
I'm not sure   a good idea   how about

A So how should we entertain our visitors?

B ¹_____ taking them to a restaurant?

A That's ²_____ ! I'm sure they'd like to try some local dishes.

C And maybe they like music. Perhaps ³_____ take them to a concert.

B ⁴_____ about that. We don't know what kind of music they like.

A Well, ⁵_____ not show them around the city? There are lots of attractions.

C I like that! ⁶_____ show them round the city and then go for dinner.

Unit 10
Price

www.longman-elt.com   www.economist.com

Pushing down prices

Keynotes

It is difficult for companies to **set the price** of a product. A lower price may help to **increase** sales, but it also **reduces** the **profit margin**. As a result, the company may have to **cut costs** to keep prices down. We often use **graphs** to show **trends** in prices over months or years. Studying the trends can help companies to choose the right **pricing strategy** for their products.

Price trends

1 What kinds of products and services are increasing in price at the moment? What things are getting cheaper?

2 Look at the graph and complete each sentence with a different item from the key.

1 Spending on _____ increased up to 1991 and then fell sharply.

2 Spending on _____ increased the most.

3 Spending on _____ rose by nearly 20 per cent.

4 Spending on _____ decreased slightly after 1996.

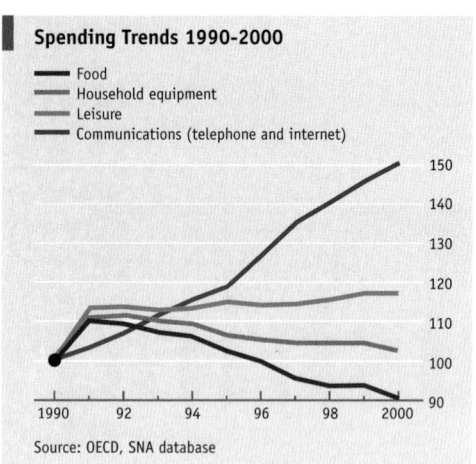

Spending Trends 1990-2000

— Food
— Household equipment
— Leisure
— Communications (telephone and internet)

150
140
130
120
110
100
90

1990 92 94 96 98 2000

Source: OECD, SNA database

How important is price to you? When you want to buy something, which do you do?

a Make sure you get good value for money?

b Spend time looking for the lowest possible price?

c Not worry about price, just buy what you want?

1 Read the article on the opposite page and match the headings 1–4 with the paragraphs a–d.

1 Big supermarkets are more efficient

2 Drinks come cheaper in large cans

3 Technology improves food production

4 Supermarkets force producers to cut costs

2 Read the article again. Are the statements true or false?

1 It costs less to produce large quantities of food than ever before.

2 Big supermarkets can offer food at lower prices because they can buy in large quantities.

3 Some food producers have reduced their range of products.

4 To meet supermarket demands, Cadbury employs more workers than before.

5 Shoppers will buy larger quantities when there is a special price.

6 For the food companies, larger portions are not much more expensive to produce.

7 The writer thinks companies will be happy to reduce the sizes of portions.

Glossary

buy in bulk buy goods in large quantities

put pressure on use your power to encourage

get a better deal get more value for your money

Survey: Food

Make it cheaper and cheaper

How technology pushes down price

a ─────────────

Prices have fallen in the food business because of advances in food production and distribution technology. Consumers have benefited greatly from those advances. People who predicted that the world would run out of food were wrong. We are producing more and more food with less and less capital. Food is therefore more plentiful and cheaper than it has ever been. Spending on food compared with other goods has fallen for many years, and continues to drop.

b ─────────────

Supermarkets have helped push down prices mainly because of their scale. Like any big business, they can invest in IT systems that make them efficient. And their size allows them to buy in bulk. As supermarkets get bigger, the prices get lower.

c ─────────────

Huge retail companies such as Wal-Mart have tremendous power and they can put pressure on producers to cut their margins. As a result, some producers have had to make cuts. In recent years, Unilever has cut its workforce by 33,000 to 245,000 and dropped lots of its minor brands as part of its "path to growth" strategy. Cadbury has shut nearly 20 per cent of its 133 factories and cut 10 per cent of its 55,000 global workforce. These cuts help keep costs down, and the price of food stays low.

d ─────────────

Does cheap food make people unhealthy? Cheap food may encourage people to eat more. Food companies certainly think that giving people more food for their money makes them buy more. Giving people bigger portions is an easy way of making them feel they have got a better deal. That is why portions have got larger and larger. In America, soft drinks came in 8oz (225g) cans in the past, then 12oz (350g), and now come in 20oz (550g) cans. If a company can sell you an 8oz portion for $7, they can sell you a 12oz portion for $8. The only extra cost to the company is the food, which probably costs 25 cents.

Now companies are under pressure to stop selling bigger portions for less money. But it is hard to change the trend. ■

Speaking   **What are the advantages and disadvantages of large chain stores and small shops? Which do you prefer to shop in?**

Match the words 1–6 from the article with the meanings a–f.

1	advances	a	the difference between the cost of production and the price of the product
2	margin	b	less important
3	workforce	c	an amount of food for one person
4	minor	d	changes that bring improvement
5	portion	e	the way a situation changes and develops
6	trend	f	all the people who work in a particular company or factory

Synonyms

Put the words and phrases in the correct column.

cut	drop	fall	lower	put up
raise	rise	reduce	push down	rocket

increase	decrease

Verbs that take an object

Look at the examples.

verb + object

1 The company has decided not to **raise** salaries this year.
2 The supermarket **raised** the price of milk.

verb – no object

3 Costs are **rising** all the time.
4 The price of milk **rose** last month.

Which of the verbs in Vocabulary 2 take an object, like 1 above?

Choose the correct verbs in *italics*.

> **The Economist**
>
> Economic trends
>
> # Earn less, spend more?
>
> **Growth slows, but consumers still spending**
>
> Consumer spending in the US [1] *rose / raised* last year, mainly because the oil companies [2] *pushed up / rose* the price of oil to the highest level for several years. Higher oil prices meant that spending on petrol for cars, as well as home heating, [3] *raised / increased*. However, salaries did not [4] *put up / go up* to match the rise in spending. Many companies [5] *cut / fell* jobs at the start of the year in order to [6] *reduce / rocket* their costs. These companies are still not [7] *increasing / rising* their workforce. Economic growth remains slow and current trends seem set to continue. ∎

Pricing strategy

A company wants to improve profitability. Which do you think is the best of the strategies below?

	Strategy	Profit increase (%)
1	Reduce costs by one per cent.	
2	Increase the volume of sales by one per cent.	
3	Increase all its prices by one per cent.	

1 Callum Taylor, a marketing expert, talks about pricing strategy on a radio programme about business. How much can a company expect to increase its profit using each of the above strategies? Listen to part one and complete the table.

2 Listen to part two and complete the sentences.

1 The cost-plus method of pricing: 'You calculate what it costs to _____ an item and then you add the _____ _____ you'd like to have.'

2 Another method: 'Find out what your _____ are ready to _____ on that product.'

3 A third way: 'Look at the _____ .'

4 Before setting a price, companies should ask two questions:
Who are the _____ _____ ?
What kind of _____ or _____ are we _____ ?

5 You shouldn't develop a product and then say: 'OK, now let's _____ _____ _____ _____ .'

Present perfect

1 Look at the examples of the present perfect and past simple. Choose the correct option in *italics* to complete the rules.

- Consumers **have benefited** greatly from advances in food production.
- In recent years, Unilever **has cut** its workforce by 33,000.
- **Has** the price of soft drinks **fallen** recently?
- The price of energy **rose** by 15 per cent last year, but it **hasn't risen** in the last 12 months.
- A year ago, the price of oil **was** $32 a barrel; now it **has reached** $52 a barrel.

1 We form the present perfect by using the past participle of the verb with *has or have / no auxiliary verb*.

2 We form present perfect questions with *has or have / do or does*.

3 We form the present perfect negative by using *hasn't or haven't / didn't*.

4 We use *the present perfect / the past simple* to talk about things that happened at a specific time in the past.

5 We use *the present perfect / the past simple* to talk about recent events and events that affect the present situation.

2 Which of the following time expressions do we usually use with the present perfect?

> in the last three months   last year   recently
> in recent years   six months ago   in 1999

For more information, see page 160.

Practice

1 Tick the correct sentences and change the incorrect ones.

1 Two years ago, we have seen big increases in the price of oil.

2 The price fell in the last two days and it is now 5 per cent lower than before.

3 Our competitors reduced their prices in January.

4 We didn't raise our prices in recent weeks: they are still at the same level as they were two months ago.

5 Have you reviewed your prices recently?

6 We have reviewed our prices in March.

2 Look at the chart and complete the text with the present perfect forms of the following verbs. Use each verb once only.

> be   double   drop   fall   rise   grow

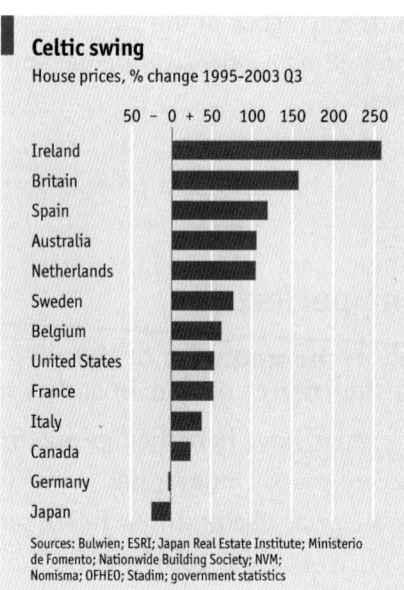

Celtic swing
House prices, % change 1995-2003 Q3

Ireland
Britain
Spain
Australia
Netherlands
Sweden
Belgium
United States
France
Italy
Canada
Germany
Japan

Sources: Bulwien; ESRI; Japan Real Estate Institute; Ministerio de Fomento; Nationwide Building Society; NVM; Nomisma; OFHEO; Stadim; government statistics

House-price index

World trends in house prices

Property is going up, but not everywhere

In the last 20 years, house prices in many countries [1] _have grown_ faster than ever before. In Ireland, house prices [2]_____ by more than 250 per cent. In Australia, the Netherlands and Spain, prices [3]_____ . However, in Germany and Japan, prices [4]_____ . Japanese house prices [5]_____ the most changeable. After huge increases during the 1980s, they [6]_____ every year in the last 12 years.

Speaking

With a partner, discuss the prices of the items below. Have these prices increased, decreased or stayed at the same level in your country in recent months?

petrol   newspapers
coffee   houses and flats
bus / train fares   shares (stock market average)

Describing a graph

People at work often have to describe graphs, figures and diagrams that show, for example, changes in price, sales or other data. The following phrases are useful for describing graphs. Match them with the graphs below and complete the missing numbers or dates.

1 *increased from 95 to* ___
2 *fell to a low point in* ___
3 *remained steady at* ___
4 *reached a peak of* ___
5 *fluctuated between* ___ *and 40*

A
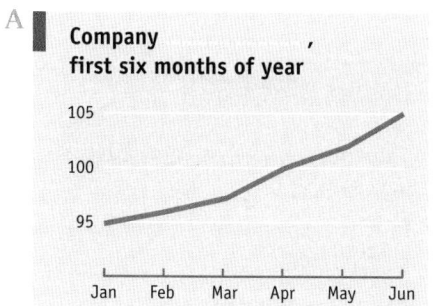
Company   ,
first six months of year

B
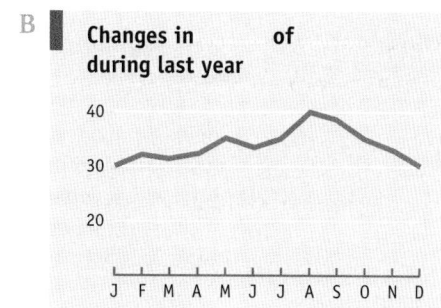
Changes in   of
during last year

C
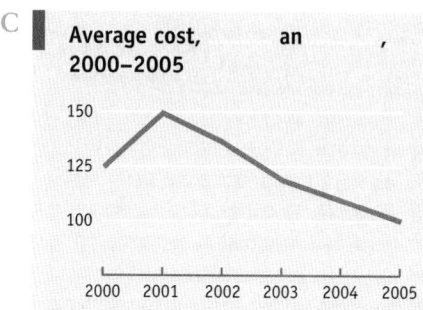
Average cost,   an   ,
2000–2005

D
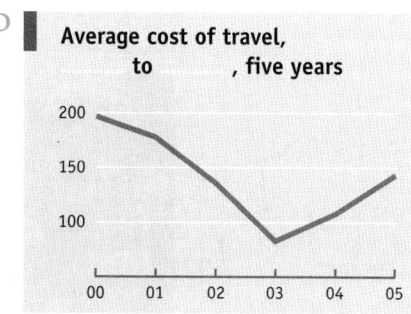
Average cost of travel,
to   , five years

E
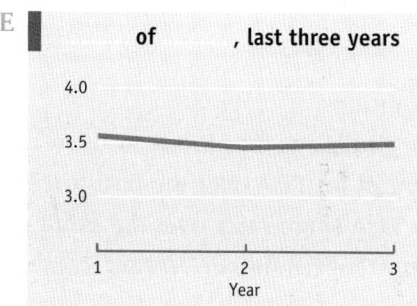
of   , last three years

Listening 2 ⊙ **1** Listen to descriptions of the five graphs and check your answers.

2 Listen again and complete the titles of the graphs.

Speaking **1** Work with a partner. Take turns to describe each of the above graphs. Start by saying what each graph shows.

2 You are going to describe a graph to your partner. Student A turn to page 139. Student B turn to page 143.

Culture at work

How much explanation?

In some cultures, people like to use a lot of detail to present information. They think it is important to explain exactly what facts and figures mean. In other cultures, people think that only a little explanation is needed to help the audience understand. How much explanation do people in your country include in presentations?

Dilemma & Decision

Dilemma: Stock market challenge

Brief

You are members of an investment group. On January 1st you invested €30,000 in shares in EU Airlines Corporation (EUA), a European airline. The share price is €1.50 and you own 20,000 shares. You also have €50,000 which you could use to buy more shares. Your task is to make as much money as you can from your investments over a year.

Guide to making money on the stock exchange

The key to making money on the stock market is to buy shares when the price is low and sell again when the price is as high as possible. But it is hard to know when the price has reached its highest point! Look at the company's profitability. When companies are making big profits, their shares usually sell at a higher price. Factors leading to share price rises: growing markets; increasing sales; cost savings. Factors leading to price falls: increasing competition, decreasing markets / sales, company debts, employment problems (strikes, etc.); rising cost of supplies.

Task 1

⊙ Work in small groups.

You will hear news bulletins for March, June and September, giving:

- the profit situation for EUA over the past three months
- changes in the EUA share price over the same period
- other factors: passenger numbers, oil price, job cuts, strikes, etc.

After each bulletin, discuss what to do. You have three choices:

1　buy more EUA shares (up to the maximum value of your cash fund)
2　sell some or all of your shares
3　take no action

Use the table to enter the value of your investments and your decision at the end of each quarter:

	Q1	Q2	Q3	Q4
Value of shares (number of shares x share price)				
Decision? buy / sell / no action				

Task 2

⊙ Listen to the news bulletin for the end of December and calculate how much money you have in shares and in cash.

How successful was your group? Did you make more or less money than other groups?

Decision:

Turn to page 146 to see the graph for the airline's share price over the year. Find out what the best decisions were and how much money you could have as a result.

Useful phrases

The share price has increased, so let's sell.

Profits have fallen – I think we should sell.

Passenger numbers are rising. Why don't we buy more shares?

Unit 11 Insurance

www.longman-elt.com www.economist.com

Honesty is the best policy

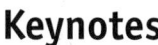

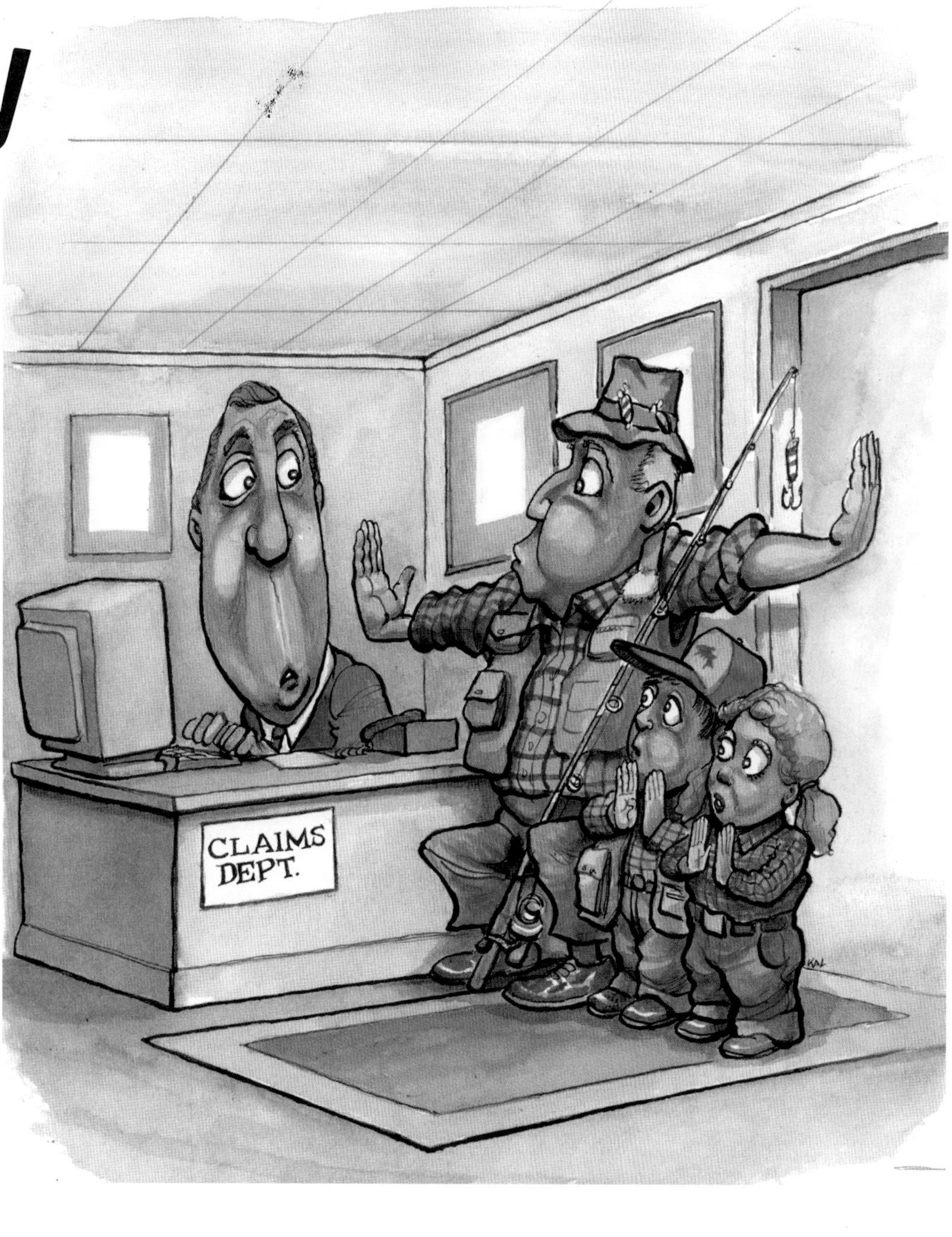

Keynotes

Many people and businesses take out insurance **policies** to **protect against** risks such as **fire, accident** and **theft**. **Policyholders** pay a yearly **premium** to the insurance company which then provides **cover against** financial loss. If something unexpected happens, the policyholder can make a **claim** and receive **compensation** for the loss or **damage**.

What insurance do you or your family have? What insurance do you have to have by law?

Read the extract from a US insurance company's website. Match the headings with paragraphs 1–4.

Auto   Home   Commercial   Life

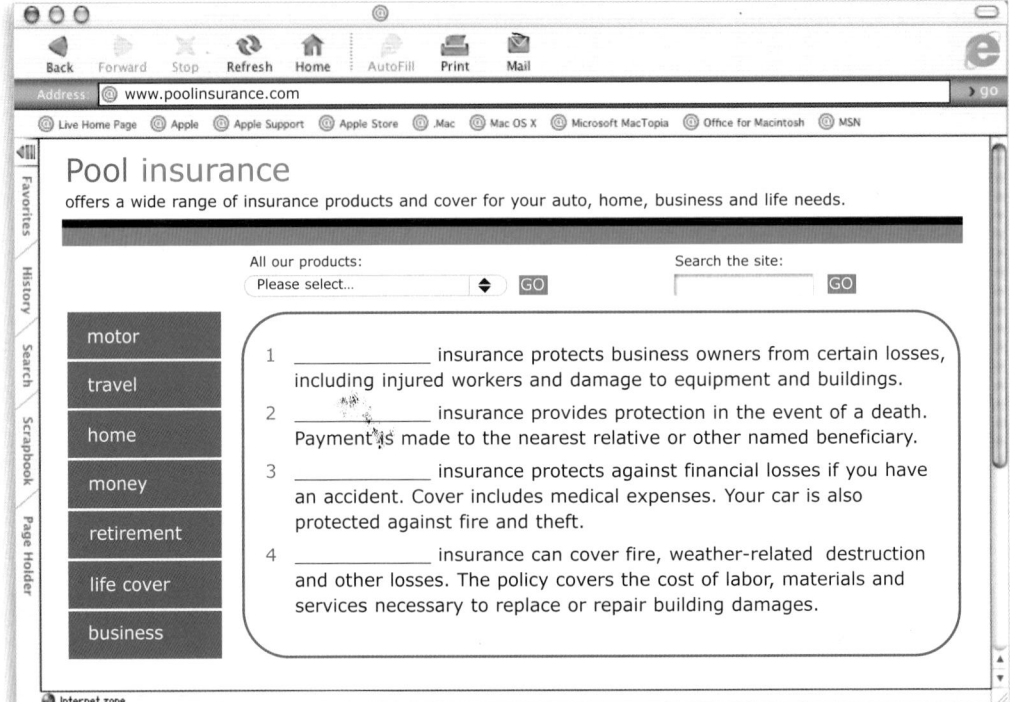

Glossary

beneficiary the person who receives the payment

auto insurance (American English) **car / motor insurance** (British English)

Pool insurance offers a wide range of insurance products and cover for your auto, home, business and life needs.

All our products: Please select...   GO   Search the site: GO

motor
travel
home
money
retirement
life cover
business

1 _____ insurance protects business owners from certain losses, including injured workers and damage to equipment and buildings.

2 _____ insurance provides protection in the event of a death. Payment is made to the nearest relative or other named beneficiary.

3 _____ insurance protects against financial losses if you have an accident. Cover includes medical expenses. Your car is also protected against fire and theft.

4 _____ insurance can cover fire, weather-related destruction and other losses. The policy covers the cost of labor, materials and services necessary to replace or repair building damages.

Speaking **Some people want to insure unusual things. Singers may insure their voice; dancers their legs. What other examples of unusual insurance cover have you heard about?**

Vocabulary 1 **Problems**

Complete the insurance claims below with the following words.

injured   damaged   destroyed   lost   stolen

'There was an accident in the factory and two people were ¹_____ . We would like to claim for their medical expenses.'

'There was a bad storm last night and our roof was ²_____ . We want to claim the cost of repairing it.'

'I'd like to claim for the theft of my car. It was ³_____ from outside my home during the night.'

'When I was on holiday last week, I ⁴_____ my wallet on the beach. I looked everywhere but couldn't find it. It had €1,000 inside!'

'We've had a fire in the computer room. All the equipment is completely ⁵_____ . We need to replace it as soon as possible.'

1 Irene Foster, an underwriter at the insurance company, Green Shield, explains how an insurance company is structured. Listen to part one and match the job activities a–f with the people who perform them 1–3.

1   manager   a   Take care of general administration.
2   clerical staff   b   Handle online and telephone applications and claims.
3   underwriters   c   Agree to accept a risk or not.
                         d   Manage staff.
                         e   Deal with the majority of applications and claims.
                         f   Take decisions on special cases.

2 Listen to part two and answer the questions.

1   What example does Irene give of a 'high risk' case? Complete the sentence: When someone has made _____ claims or more in _____ .

2   What example does Irene give of a case where the company may 'review the situation'?

3   What special terms does the company sometimes offer in cases of high risk? Complete the sentence: We may quote a _____ premium or offer only limited _____ .

Vocabulary 2 Insurance

Match the words 1–6 with the meanings a–f.

1   administration   a   a request to your insurance company to pay for damage or loss
2   department   b   the amount you pay for insurance during a particular period
3   claim   c   the conditions of an agreement or contract
4   premium   d   tell a customer how much something will cost
5   quote   e   managing or organising the work of a company
6   terms   f   a part, or section, of a company where people do a particular kind of work.

Vocabulary 3 Insurance fraud

Many people make fraudulent claims on their insurance. Which of the following actions can be described as fraud?

1   Being honest about the value of your financial losses.
2   Making a dishonest claim for an injury you don't have.
3   Lying about how much cash was in the wallet you lost.
4   Telling the truth about the cost of a car that was stolen.
5   Claiming that the repair cost was more expensive than it really was.
6   Making a legitimate claim for items destroyed by fire.

1 **Read the article and answer the questions.**

1 How much does insurance fraud cost in the US?

2 What two kinds of technology can be used to identify fraud?

3 How much has Highway Insurance saved as a result of using this technology?

2 **Complete the text with the following sentences.**

A The tremors can indicate that they are not telling the truth.

B 'If a fraudulent policyholder decides to opt out, we are happy that their claim just goes away,' says Lawrence.

C 'Now we are able to pass these savings along to our genuine customers.'

D With VRA, the company is now able to identify that nearly one in five auto theft claims are fraudulent.

E But most often, no one's going to find out if an average consumer stretches the truth a bit.

FIGHTING FRAUD

INSURANCE FRAUD costs Americans $80 billion a year – $950 per family. This is not just because of large-scale fraud – everyday consumers also contribute to the loss by making dishonest claims. ¹____ A new lie detector telephone technology may change that. The Layered Voice Analyzer (LVA) measures micro tremors in the voice to determine the emotional state of speakers. ²____

A similar system, the Voice Risk Analyzer (VRA), is already in use in the UK and has helped UK companies to make savings. Highway Insurance is a UK-based auto underwriter that uses the VRA in their fraud detection programs. Michael Lawrence, marketing and special projects manager with the company, reports that only 5 per cent of claims for auto theft were thought to be fraudulent before using the system. ³____

'The analysis takes place in our first stage of screening,' says Lawrence. The process begins when a policyholder reports a claim to the company's automated telephone system. The system informs policyholders that their calls may be monitored for fraud-prevention and detection purposes. If the voice analysis readings show a claim to be suspicious, the policyholder is informed that further investigation is required. A live telephone interview is then arranged. VRA readings show that 38 per cent of claims relating to theft are high risk, and 18 per cent are eventually found to be fraudulent.

If policyholders withdraw their claim during the investigation process, the company will take no action. ⁴____ As a result of fewer claims and more accurate identification of fraud, Highway Insurance has saved more than £3 million. 'Before we started using this technology, we didn't know how much fraudulent claims cost us, because we didn't know which claims were fraudulent,' explains Lawrence. ⁵____

Glossary

stretch the truth make something seem more important or bigger than it really is

tremors shaking voice that you can't control

emotional state the way someone feels (e.g. worried, afraid, confident)

suspicious possibly dishonest or fraudulent

Choose the best word a–c to complete the sentences.

1 The company _____ all claims to see which ones could be fraudulent.
   a screens   b detects   c determines

2 Calls are _____ using the Voice Risk Analyzer.
   a controlled   b maintained   c monitored

3 If any calls are suspicious, the company _____ them.
   a invents   b invests   c investigates

4 The VRA system helps to _____ fraud.
   a prohibit   b prevent   c protect

5 People often _____ fraudulent claims when they hear that the company will investigate them.
   a contribute   b withdraw   c identify

6 Identifying fraudulent claims has helped the company to _____ money.
   a raise   b spend   c save

Honesty quiz

Which of these dishonest actions is most serious? Put them in order from the most to the least serious.

1 Your neighbour ordered some pizza but it is delivered to your address by mistake. You eat the pizza and say nothing to your neighbour.

2 You spend €15 on some shopping for a friend. You tell your friend that you spent €20.

3 A shop assistant gives you change for €50 when you only gave a €20 note. You say nothing.

4 You find a €100 note in the changing room at the swimming pool. You keep it.

5 You order 12 bottles of wine from an online distributor. The company sends you 24 bottles by mistake. You don't tell them about the mistake.

6 You claim €750 on your insurance policy for personal things stolen from your apartment. The real value was only €200.

Passives

Look at the examples of active and passive sentences. Choose the best alternatives in *italics* in the rules below.

Active: The policyholder **reports** a claim.

Passive:

- A claim **is reported** by the policyholder.
- If the claim is suspicious, the policyholder **is informed** and a live telephone interview **is arranged**.
- Eighteen per cent of claims **are found** to be fraudulent.
- Your claim **is being considered** and a decision will be taken shortly.
- My car **has been stolen!**
- Three houses **were destroyed** by the storm.

1   The passive is formed by using the correct tense of the verb *to be / to have* with the past participle of the verb (e.g. *found, stolen*).

2   We more commonly use the *active / passive* form of the verb when it is important to say who performed the action, or what was responsible for the event.

3   The *active / passive* form of the verb is usually used when we don't know who or what was responsible.

4   When passive sentences include information about the agent (who or what was responsible for the action), we use *by / for* with the agent.

 For more information, see page 160.

Practice   **1 Rewrite the sentences below using the correct form of the passive. Omit the agent if it isn't important.**

1   Howard Baines set up the company in 1978.
2   To begin with, Baines and his directors divided the company into three departments.
3   Since then, they have restructured the company into five departments.
4   A manager heads each department.
5   The company now employs 4,000 people.
6   They are building a new head office for 2,000 staff.
7   They will complete the new building next month.

2 Complete the article with the appropriate passive form of the verbs in brackets.

Insurance companies see manual workers as high risk

Low paid manual workers (¹charge) _____ 10 to 20 per cent more for their motor insurance than high-earning professional people, according to data from the Automobile Association. One man (²quote) _____ £713 for car insurance when he gave his job as IT consultant. But when the same person, with the same car and address gave his job as factory worker, he (³offer) _____ cover for a cost of £793.

So what are the best and worst jobs for car insurers? The highest rates (⁴attract) _____ by high-earning sportsmen, because they often drive fast, expensive cars. Nightclub staff (⁵see) _____ as high risk because they park their cars in areas of high crime at night. At the other end of the scale, the lowest premiums (⁶pay) _____ by accountants. They (⁷believe) _____ to be careful people who take few risks when driving.

Expressing arguments

In business, as in other areas of life, we often have to make difficult decisions. The best way to decide is to look at all the arguments for and against and to see which is the strongest argument. The following phrases are useful for putting forward arguments and responding.

The fact is ... , so ... ☑	Yes, but ... ☑
My view is ... , because ... ☑	I understand your point, but ... ☑
Surely the main point is ... ☑	On the other hand ... ☑
You have to consider ... ☑	That's right. ☑
Don't you think ... ? ☑	

Listening 2 ⊙

1 Irene, Jane and Mike are three underwriters at Green Shield Insurance Company. They are arguing about a special case: a man who has a criminal conviction for theft has applied for insurance cover for his house. Should the company offer him insurance? Listen to the discussion. How many people are for offering the man insurance?

2 Listen again. Tick the phrases you hear in the list above.

Speaking

Discuss the questions in pairs. Practice putting arguments for and against the idea.

1   What do you think of the case in Listening 2? Should the company insure the man's house?

2   Should insurance companies cover the medical expenses of people who smoke a lot or drink a lot?

Culture at work

To interrupt or not?

What are meetings like in your country? Does everyone try to speak at the same time? Or are there a lot of silences? In some cultures, people think it is a sign of respect to take time before responding to what others say. In other cultures, people are uncomfortable about silence. They normally respond immediately, or even interrupt another speaker to give their own idea.

Dilemma & Decision

Dilemma: A fair decision?

Brief

You are members of the Financial Ombudsman Service – an independent organisation that helps to settle disagreements between companies and their customers. You have been asked to look at the following dispute between a car owner and an insurance company following the theft of a car.

Jane Buxton was at a restaurant in the city centre when her handbag was stolen. Inside the bag were her house keys, car keys, wallet and driving licence with her home address on it. She reported the theft to the police and to her insurance company. The police advised her to change the locks on her house. But ten days later, her car was stolen from outside her house. She made a claim on her motor insurance policy, but the company refused to settle the claim. They told her she was at fault because she didn't change the locks on her car after her handbag was stolen. Jane thinks this is unfair and the company should settle her claim.

Task 1

Work in two groups. Group A, read the arguments for the insurance company's decision. Group B, read Jane Buxton's point of view. Group A turn to page 139. Group B turn to page 143.

Task 2

Should the company settle the claim? Meet with two students from the other group and put forward the different arguments for and against. Discuss the arguments from an objective point of view and try to find a satisfactory solution.

Write it up

As the ombudsman, write a letter to the insurance company. Tell them either that you support their decision not to settle the claim, or that you think it was an unfair decision and they should settle. Explain your arguments.

Decision:

⊙ Now listen to Carl Herring, a member of the Financial Ombudsman Service explaining the decision of the Ombudsman.

Useful phrases

The fact is ..., so ...
Surely the main point is ...
My view is ..., because ...
On the other hand ...

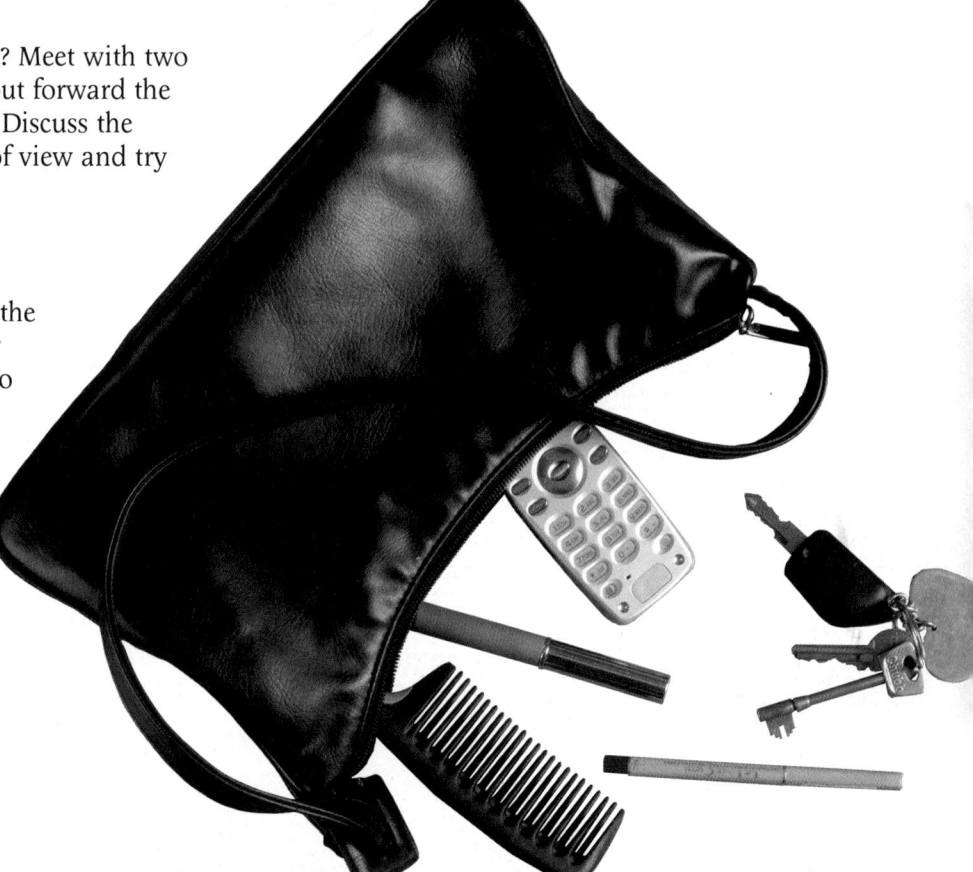

Unit 12
Service

www.longman-elt.com   www.economist.com

A complaint is a gift

Keynotes

Customer satisfaction is an important part of a company's sales strategy, so companies try to provide **good customer service**. That means offering **high quality** products and services, answering **queries**, making it easy for customers to order and **pay for** goods, and **delivering** on time. Companies also need to have a system for **handling complaints**, so that if they make a mistake or offer **poor service**, they can **deal with** the problem. Most companies **train** their customer service staff to deal politely with customers.

Complaining

In which of these situations should the customer complain? If not, why not?

1 The food in a restaurant is overcooked.

2 You don't like the music in a café.

3 You wait ten minutes to be served in a shop.

4 There is cigarette ash on the floor of an expensive hotel room.

5 Your train is five minutes late.

6 After ordering a book online, the wrong book is sent. You send it back but after three weeks, the right book still hasn't arrived.

7 A car hire firm didn't provide maps of the local roads.

Feedback on service

Complete the comments to a holiday travel company with the following words.

apology	dissatisfied	friendly	pleased	wrong	excellent
useful	mistake	dirty	rude	poor	

We had ¹_____ service from first enquiries on the telephone to arrival at the resort. Staff very ²_____ and efficient.

Very ³_____ to receive the receipt and confirmation the day after booking.

We were very ⁴_____ with the service at the hotel. Our room was ⁵_____ and the hotel receptionist was ⁶_____ .

When I booked my holiday, your representative quoted me the ⁷_____ price. I pointed out the ⁸_____ , but she made no ⁹_____ .

The holiday representative had good local knowledge and gave ¹⁰_____ information.

The service in the hotel restaurant was ¹¹_____ .

1 Read the article on the opposite page and choose the sentence, a or b, that best describes the main point.

a Companies that receive no complaints offer the best service.

b It's good for companies to receive complaints.

2 Read the article again. Are the statements true or false?

1 Australians are correct when they say that the British complain too much.
2 The British aren't very direct when they make complaints.
3 Americans only complain when there is a big problem.
4 British companies don't spend much on service.
5 The Marriott Hotel Group trains its staff to follow a fixed routine when handling complaints.
6 Complaining about bad service in Britain doesn't bring any results.

Glossary

whinge complain (informal)

pom (Aus) a person from Britain (informal)

make a fuss become angry about something

in a roundabout way not in a direct way

phlegmatic always calm, not getting angry or excited

Customer service
Getting better service

The failure to complain is everywhere

Australians call the British "whingeing Poms" because they complain so much. But a new study suggests that Brits should whinge more, not less. A team led by Chris Voss of the London Business School found that service quality in Britain is typically worse than in America. One reason, the research suggests, is that British customers complain less about bad service than hard-to-please Americans do.

The failure to complain is everywhere in Britain. Hunter Hansen, an American who runs the Marriott Hotel in London's Grosvenor Square, notes that a British guest would make a fuss only about a significant problem—and even then, would do so in a roundabout way. Americans are critical of even small mistakes.

The result, Mr Voss finds, is that Brits suffer. But so do companies in Britain's service industries: they do not receive much feedback, and so lose a chance to improve service quality. Indeed, they may spend more than they need on service-quality improvements, because they do not get direct help from customers.

Management gurus know more about how companies respond to complaints than about why the British are phlegmatic. In America, well-run companies have "service recovery" strategies. Staff at the Marriott Group are trained in the LEARN routine— Listen, Empathise, Apologise, React, Notify. The final step ensures that there is a record of each complaint. The Ritz-Carlton hotel chain, another with a good reputation for handling complaints from customers, trains its staff not just to say "sorry" but "please accept my apology" and gives them a budget to reimburse angry guests.

When Brits finally complain, they get what they want. Mr Voss told his doctor that he would like to have the results of tests more quickly. "The next time, I got them sooner," he says, in surprise. ■

The Economist

Speaking **1** Do people in your country complain a lot? What about?

2 How would you describe the quality of service in your country?

Dealing with complaints

Match the steps 1–5 from the LEARN routine with the explanations a–e.

1	LISTEN	**a**	Show that you understand how the customer is feeling.
2	EMPATHISE	**b**	Tell management about the problem.
3	APOLOGISE	**c**	Don't interrupt when the customer explains the problem.
4	REACT	**d**	Promise to do something.
5	NOTIFY	**e**	Say 'Sorry'.

Synonyms

Choose the word or phrase that has a similar meaning to the ones in *italics*.

1   It's a *significant* problem and a lot of people are complaining about it.
   a   minor   b   typical   c   important

2   Our business is *suffering* as a result of poor service.
   a   doing badly   b   recovering   c   failing

3   If the service is poor, the company will *reimburse you.*
   a   ask you for money   b   recover the money   c   refund your money

4   The hotel has a *good reputation.*
   a   has had a good report   b   is known to be very good   c   is very expensive

Collocations

1 Cross out the noun in each group which does not go with the verb.

1	make	a complaint / a customer / an apology
2	deal with	a service / a customer / a problem
3	handle	a query / a need / a complaint
4	offer	a refund / an apology / a complaint
5	satisfy	a need / a customer / a complaint

2 Choose the correct verbs in *italics* to complete the text.

If a company doesn't [1]*satisfy / offer* a customer's needs and he or she [2]*makes / offers* a complaint, the company should respond immediately and [3]*deal with / satisfy* the customer's problem. Businesses that don't try to [4]*satisfy / handle* their customers usually receive more complaints. If the company [5]*offers / deals with* a refund, the complaining customer will often come back. But if the company fails to even [6]*make / handle* an apology, the customer will not only change to another company, but may also tell other people about their bad experience.

1 **What do you think customer service staff should do in the following situations? Match the situations 1–5 with the actions a–e.**

1 A customer is angry about a mistake.

2 An angry customer describes the problem.

3 A customer complains but doesn't demand any action.

4 A customer demands action but the company can't do what the customer wants.

5 The customer is a very difficult person.

a Suggest a solution.

b Say what you can do.

c Stay calm.

d Accept that you probably won't find a solution.

e Listen carefully and repeat to check.

2 **Now listen to an extract from a training seminar for customer service staff and check your answers to exercise 1.**

3 **Listen to the trainer again and answer the questions.**

1 What do employees often think when a customer shouts at them?

2 What do you think it means 'to solve the problem professionally'?

3 Which word makes the customer feel confident that the employee is going to do something? Which words should the staff *not* use?

Language check

Conditional 1

Study the following examples. Complete the rules below with *present* or *future*.

– If the customer **doesn't demand** action, **you'll have to** suggest a solution.

– If **it's** a difficult person, you probably **won't** find a solution.

– If we **make** a mistake, **we'll** correct it.

– If we **ask** the customers for feedback, we **can find out** what they want.

– Most people **will be** satisfied if you **apologise**.

– If you **can't replace** the product, **will you give** me a refund?

1 In the first conditional, the verb following *if* is in the _____ tense.

2 The verb in the other half of the sentence refers to the _____ and is generally formed with *will*.

3 We use the first conditional to talk about the _____ result of a possible action or event.

Note: If the result is not certain, we use *can* or *could* instead of *will*, meaning 'It's possible'.

 For more information, see page 160.

Practice

1 Look at the payment terms below. Write sentences linking the possible actions and events with the future results. Use conditional 1.

Possible action or event	➤	Future result
You pay within 10 days	➤	you receive a discount

If you pay within 10 days, you will receive a discount.

Possible action or event	➤	Future result
1 You pay by credit card	➤	we add a charge of 2 per cent to your bill
2 We don't receive payment by the due date	➤	we charge interest at 2.5 per cent a month
3 You request delivery within 24 hours	➤	there is an additional charge of €20
4 You decide not to keep the product	➤	we refund your money in full

2 Complete the extracts from company brochures with the present simple or future form of the verbs in brackets.

Lowest prices guaranteed!

If you (¹find) _____ the same product at a lower price in another store, we (²refund) _____ the difference.

Customer service guarantee

If you (³be) _____ dissatisfied in any way with the quality of our service, we (⁴send) _____ you a €15 voucher.

Special offer!

We (⁵deduct) _____ 10 per cent from the price if you (⁶order) _____ before October 31st.

Cancellation charges

If you (⁷cancel) _____ less than four weeks before the date of departure, the total cost of travel (⁸be) _____ payable.

Product information

If you (⁹require) _____ further information about any of the products featured in this brochure, please call 040 900 900 and our sales staff (¹⁰be) _____ pleased to help you.

Speaking

1 Work in pairs. Look at the alternatives below. Describe the result of taking each action.

If I stay at home, I'll save money.

Go out with friends this evening or stay at home and study?

Buy a new mobile phone / coat / bag or keep the one I've got?

Buy a book online or in a bookshop?

Look for a job abroad or work in my own country?

2 Think of some real situations where you have to decide between two or more possible actions. Talk about them with your partner using *If ... , I'll ...* .

Dealing with problems

When you have a problem, you have to look at all the possible options and find the best solution. The following phrases are useful for discussing problems. Match the five steps in problem-solving with the phrases a–e.

Step 1: *Explain the problem*

Step 2: *Present the options*

Step 3: *Consider the result of each option*

Step 4: *Choose the best solution*

Step 5: *Promise action*

a *If you (do X), it will mean ...*

b *I'll arrange ...*

c *It's better/ best if I (do Y).*

d *I've got a problem ...*

e *There are two possibilities: you could either (do X) or you could (do Y).*

Listening 2 **Magda Zawadski phones Shane, the customer service rep of a UK supplier, about a problem with the delivery of some machine components. Listen and answer the questions.**

1 What is Magda's problem?

2 What two options does Shane present?

3 Which option does Magda choose and why?

4 What does Shane promise to do?

Speaking **1 Work in pairs. Role-play the phone call between Magda and Shane.**

2 Role-play two situations involving a shop manager and a supplier.

Student A give Student B this information.

Situation 1: Shop manager

Your shop sells fruit and vegetables. You received some tomatoes this morning but they are damaged and you can't sell them. Phone the supplier. Explain the problem, listen to the options and choose the best solution.

Situation 2: Supplier

Your company supplies bread to stores. You receive a phone call from a shop manager. Listen to the customer and offer two possible options:

1 – offer to collect all the extra rolls.

2 – tell the shop to sell what they can. Refund the cost of any rolls that they don't sell.

Listen to the shop manager's decision and promise action.

Student B turn to page 146.

Culture at work ## Showing emotion

If you feel angry about poor service or bad mistakes at work, do you show your anger? Or do you try to stay calm? When you complain, is it better to show how you feel, or to present the facts in a quiet, neutral way? In some cultures, people accept strong emotions as normal; in other cultures, people think it is not appropriate to show emotions in business situations. Which culture do you belong to?

Dilemma & Decision

Dilemma: Service not included

Brief

You are the senior managers at House & Home, a chain of warehouse-style stores selling furniture and fittings for the home. The company is suffering. Competition from other similar stores is strong and sales are falling. You think that the main reason for the loss of sales is poor customer service. To find out more about the problem, you asked your customers for feedback. The following complaints were the most common:

- Staff gave wrong information.
- Staff didn't know anything about the products.
- Staff were not interested in my query.
- Staff were rude.
- Sales staff were busy talking to each other.
- It was difficult to find help even when the store wasn't busy.

You believe that if you can offer better service than your competitors, the customers will return. The question is: how can you improve service? There are three possible options:

1 Recruit more staff for each store.
2 Improve staff training.
3 Offer higher pay to sales staff.

Task 1

Work in three groups. Find out more about one of the options and the possible results of choosing this option.

Group A turn to page 139. Group B turn to page 144.
Group C turn to page 146.

Task 2

Form new groups including members of A, B and C. Share the information you have and discuss the three possible options. Choose the best solution and present your choice to the other groups.

Write it up

Write a short report for the Directors of House & Home. Use the following headings:
Brief summary of the problem
Possible options (bullet points)
Best solution

Decision:

⊙ Now listen to Mandy Dunwoody, the Human Resources Director at House & Home, explaining how the company solved the problem of poor customer service.

Useful phrases

The problem is …
We could either … or …
If we (do X), we will / won't …
I think the best solution is to …

Review 4

Language check

The present perfect

Complete the text with the present perfect form of the following verbs (positive or negative).

be   decide   fall   introduce   rise   see   stay

The Channel Tunnel is an impressive example of modern technology, but it [1]_____ so successful as a financial venture. Shareholders are unhappy about the latest reports, which show that the number of cars using the tunnel [2]_____ by 8 per cent in the last twelve months. The number of trucks and commercial vehicles [3]_____ at the same level, but the company [4]_____ an increase in its market share. Airline traffic between London and Paris [5]_____ because of low cost airfares. Eurotunnel's directors [6]_____ not to review their pricing strategy. Instead, they [7]_____ a programme of cost-cutting in the hope of saving the company.

Passives

Rewrite the sentences in the passive.

1 We describe the results of this survey in our latest report.
   The results ...

2 They call the new model the 'Robomat'.
   The new model ...

3 They are building a new office block in the city centre.
   A new office ...

4 They will complete the building next year.
   The building ...

5 The company has developed a new drink.
   A new drink ...

6 The company raised salaries by 4 per cent last year.
   Salaries ...

7 The company offered a job to only one person.
   Only one person ...

8 The company manufactures the T408 in Germany.
   The T408 ...

Conditional 1

Complete the sentences with the correct form of the verbs in brackets.

1 If you have an accident, the insurance company (pay) _____ the costs.

2 If you (not have) _____ insurance, you will have to pay for the damage yourself.

3 You could miss your plane if you (not hurry) _____ .

4 You (not lose) _____ money if you invest in a strong company.

5 There will be an extra charge if the customer (not pay) _____ on time.

6 The company (need) _____ to recruit more staff if they set up the new office.

7 Our staff (learn) _____ to do a better job if we give them training.

8 If the quality (be) _____ poor, our customers will complain.

Consolidation

Choose the correct form of the word or phrase in _italics_.

Everyone thinks British food is the worst in the world. But it [1]_improved / has improved_ a lot in recent years. Britons [2]_found / have found_ a new interest in food. If you [3]_read / will read_ British newspapers, you will see recipes and restaurant reviews. New restaurants [4]_is / are_ being advertised everywhere. Cooking programmes [5]_schedule / are scheduled_ on TV every night and kitchens [6]_became / have become_ bigger and better.

The biggest change that can [7]_see / be seen_ is in the quality of produce in shops. Twenty years ago, there [8]_was / has been_ only one kind of tomato in supermarkets. Now, if you [9]_visit / will visit_ a British supermarket, you can find 15 types of tomato. A similar change [10]_has took / has taken_ place in other rich countries. And in developing countries, it [11]_has reported / has been reported_ that there is a lot more food available to the poor.

But the wrong kind of food [12]_was / is being_ consumed too. In some countries, more than half the population is overweight. Doctors warn that if people [13]_won't / don't_ eat better, there [14]_are / will be_ more deaths from over-eating than from smoking.

Vocabulary check

1 Choose the best option a–c to complete the text.

John went skiing last winter. He had an
¹_____ and fell 20 metres down the
mountain. He wasn't ²_____ , but his camera
was ³_____ . The cost of repairs was €200.
He tried to ⁴_____ on his travel insurance,
but the insurance company said that his
⁵_____ didn't cover dangerous sports.

1	a accident	b	incident	c	injury
2	a damaged	b	unhealthy	c	injured
3	a injured	b	damaged	c	destroyed
4	a complain	b	cover	c	claim
5	a protection	b	policy	c	claim

2 Choose the best option a–c to complete the text.

Online shopping has increased dramatically in
recent years as more and more people use the
internet to ¹_____ travel tickets and buy
goods. However, there can be problems when
buying online. Some retailers have found it
difficult to guarantee ²_____ times: goods
may arrive late or not at all. Some customers
become frustrated when they are unable to cancel
an order or get a ³_____ for goods they don't
want. Companies that try to ⁴_____
spending on customer service may find it
difficult to ⁵_____ all the complaints from
⁶_____ customers.

1	a book	b	require	c	command
2	a delivery	b	distribution	c	service
3	a payback	b	return	c	refund
4	a reduce	b	put down	c	fall
5	a apologise	b	deal	c	handle
6	a satisfied	b	dissatisfied	c	unsatisfied

Career skills

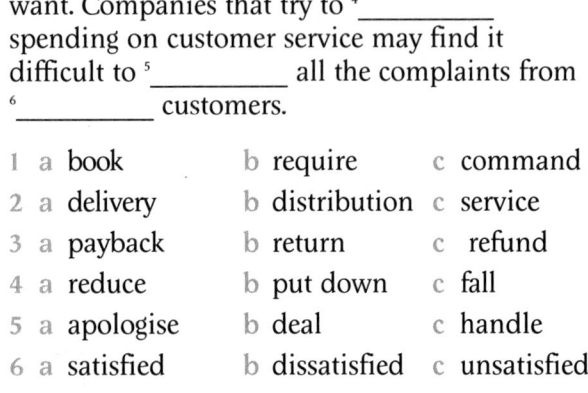

Unemployment rate 1998–2005
% of total workforce

Choose the correct phrase to complete each sentence describing the graph.

dropped from 6% to 4.5%   fell to   fluctuated
remained steady   reached a peak

1 From 1998 to 2000, the unemployment rate
_____ between 4.0 and 4.3 per cent.
2 In 2000, the rate _____ 3.1 per cent.
3 The level of unemployment _____ during
the next two years.
4 In 2004, unemployment _____ of
6.0 per cent.
5 In the second half of 2004, the rate
_____ .

Expressing arguments

**A and B discuss whether to hire a big room
or a smaller room for a party for customers.
They don't know how many people will
attend. Match the phrases with the
arguments a–e.**

A My view is that we should hire the big room,
B On the other hand,
A I understand your point,
B Surely the main point
A That's right.

a If the room is too small, our customers will
leave – and that could cost us a lot!
b but if a lot of people come, we will need the
space.
c is to save costs where we can.
d because it's better to have too much space
than not enough.
e we might have to pay a lot of money for space
we don't need.

Dealing with problems

**An office worker (A) phones a technician (B).
Put the dialogue in the correct order.**

B OK, but if we send someone to you, you may
have to wait till this afternoon.
B Fine. Then I'll arrange for someone to come to
you.
A I've got a problem with my laptop – it isn't
working.
A That's OK, I can wait.
B Right. Well there are two possibilities: we
could send someone to you to look at it, or
you could bring it to us.
A I can't bring it to you very easily – it's
connected to other equipment at my desk.

Unit 13
Productivity

www.longman-elt.com   www.economist.com

Fighting back

Keynotes

In manufacturing, productivity means the **amount** of goods produced in relation to the work, time and money needed to produce them. There are many ways for companies to **improve** productivity: by installing new equipment with more **up-to-date technology**, for example. Many manufacturers and suppliers have a system of **just-in-time delivery**, which reduces the cost of carrying large quantities of **stock**. More generally, productivity means doing something efficiently: not **wasting** time and **resources**.

Increasing productivity

Which of the following factors can help to increase productivity for manufacturers, and which can reduce productivity?

- ☐ delays in delivery of components
- ☐ up-to-date technology
- ☐ effective quality control
- ☐ products that fail quality tests
- ☐ out-of-date technology

- ☐ robots
- ☐ shortage of staff
- ☐ efficient suppliers
- ☐ good workers

Listening 1 ⊙

1 Listen to Paul Gardner, Managing Director of a chemicals company, Absolute Solvents, talking about what productivity means in his business. Tick the factors above that he talks about. Which two factors have helped to improve productivity at Absolute Solvents, and which two have been problems?

2 Listen again and answer the questions.

1 Why is productivity an important concept in Paul's business?
2 What factor does he say is 'vital'?
3 What can happen if there's a problem with the process?
4 What does Paul say is 'the biggest problem'?
5 What problems can there be with people?
6 What does Paul say is 'essential to high productivity'?

Speaking

Do you think the same factors could help to increase productivity in the car industry?

Reading

1 Read the article on the opposite page and decide if the following statements are true or false.

1 Car manufacturers can't produce enough to meet customer demands.
2 Models need to be updated more often.
3 Each car factory can only produce one model.
4 Productivity is very high.
5 It takes too long to deliver finished cars to the customer.
6 Sales forecasts are accurate.
7 Manufacturers could save money by building cars to order.
8 The car industry probably won't change much in the next few years.

2 A number of factors increase manufacturing costs and reduce profits. Which of the following are mentioned in the article?

1 developing a wide range of models
2 high labour costs
3 holding components in stock
4 holding stocks of finished goods
5 price discounts
6 strikes

Glossary

over-capacity when an industry is capable of producing more than it needs to

segment a particular part of the market (e.g. luxury cars, sports utility vehicles)

order-to-delivery cycle the usual time between the customer placing an order and receiving the product

assembly the process of putting the parts together to build a finished product

Car manufacturing

Revolution in the car industry

Car factories of the future will be smaller and cleaner, and not all owned by car companies

The car business has a serious problem: it is producing too many cars. This over-capacity is resulting in fierce competition. Each manufacturer is competing in every segment of the market, with a huge range of models to attract different consumers. And models are frequently updated to keep interest fresh. This is making the business complex and expensive. So how can companies cut costs and increase their profit margins?

To offer so many different models, car companies need factories that are completely flexible. They need to switch quickly from making one model to another to meet changing demands. Honda was first to do this, organising its factories so that any one of them could make any model of car. They can switch to a new model overnight, simply by changing the software in the robots.

Delivery is another issue that affects margins. For years, companies have tried to cut the time between a customer placing an order for a car and taking delivery. Manufacturers now operate a just-in-time production system. The components for each car arrive at precisely the right moment when they are needed on the assembly line. Such production methods have cut the cost of holding components in stock, and have resulted in high productivity. Most makers are now able to assemble a car in just 18–20 man-hours.

But once the car is finished, it usually stays in a distribution centre for 40–80 days. A shorter order-to-delivery cycle would lower the costs of holding stocks of finished cars. Moreover, most of these vehicles need to be discounted to get people to buy them. With big discounts on sale price, there is no guarantee of profits even when the factories are busy.

The magic answer to all this could be "build to order" (BTO). Instead of following the sales department's forecasts, cars could be quickly assembled to the customer's orders. Nissan has calculated they could increase profit by as much as $3,600 a vehicle in this way.

But some people in the industry predict that the shape of car manufacturing will change even more radically. One view is that today's manufacturers will disappear. In their place will be vehicle brand owners (or VBOs). They will do only the designing, engineering and marketing of vehicles. Everything else, including even final assembly, will be done by the parts suppliers.

Such changes to the way the industry is organised may be necessary if companies are to survive. ∎

Speaking

What are the advantages and disadvantages of BTO for the manufacturers? Would you prefer to choose a car from the ones that your local dealer has in stock, or to order a car with your choice of colour and features? What features would you choose to have? (e.g. satellite navigation, air conditioning, CD-player ... ?)

Design to delivery

Match the words 1–8 with the meanings a–h.

1	delay	a	change from one thing to another
2	demand	b	a set of similar products made by a particular company
3	forecast	c	a situation where something is late
4	model	d	a prediction about a future situation
5	range	e	people's need or wish to buy particular goods
6	stock	f	make something more modern, using the latest technology
7	switch	g	a type or design of car or machine
8	update	h	a supply of items that a company keeps to use when it needs them

Just-in-time production

Study the diagram and complete the labels, 1–5, with these words.

assembly   components   finished goods   order   supplier

1 Manufacturers _____ supplies electronically according to need.

2 _____ delivers parts to the manufacturer several times a day.

3 _____ are taken to the assembly-line at the moment they are needed.

4 _____ of parts to build the finished product.

5 Stocks of _____ wait for delivery to the customer.

Word building

Complete the tables.

Noun	Person	Verb
production, product	1 _____	2 _____
3 _____	---	deliver
supply	4 _____	5 _____
manufacturing	6 _____	7 _____

Noun	Adjective
productivity	8 _____
9 _____	efficient

Efficient stock control

Complete the text with words from Vocabulary sections 1–3.

Manufacturing businesses hold stocks of [1]_____ to be used in the assembly process. If a [2]_____ fails to deliver parts on time, the company can use its stocks to avoid a [3]_____ in production. Companies also hold stocks of [4]_____ that are waiting to be sold. Without these, the company could lose sales if customer [5]_____ unexpectedly increases. But holding [6]_____ costs money so that's why companies [7]_____ the minimum quantity for their needs, and arrange [8]_____ just in time.

Gavin Floyd is Production Improvement Manager at a company that manufactures inks for printing. Listen to him talking about his work and answer the questions.

1   What is Gavin's main job?
2   What do companies use Six Sigma for?
3   What can a Six Sigma analysis show?
4   What three types of waste does Six Sigma help to reduce?

Adjectives and adverbs

1 Study the examples. Which one contains an adjective? What is the difference between an adjective and an adverb? Which adverbs describe *how* you do something, and which describe *how often*?

–   Over-capacity in the car industry is resulting in fierce competition.
–   Models are frequently updated.
–   Cars can be assembled quickly to customers' orders.
–   Honda can switch production easily between models.
–   Cars usually stay in distribution centres for some time.
–   Supplies are ordered electronically, by computer.
–   Everyone is working hard to finish the project on time.
–   Our staff work well as a team.

2 Complete the rules.

1   We usually form adverbs by adding these two letters to the adjective: _____ .
2   When the adjective ends in -*y*, we form the adverb with _____ .
3   When the adjective ends in -*ic*, we form the adverb with _____ .
4   *Good*, *hard* and *fast* are adjectives. Their adverb forms are irregular. What are they?

3 Choose the correct answer for each question.

1   Where do we usually place adverbs that describe *how*?
    in front of the main verb / at the end of the sentence
2   Where do we usually place adverbs that describe *how often*?
    in front of the main verb / at the end of the sentence

 For more information, see page 161.

1 Complete the text with adverbs formed from these adjectives.

| ~~efficient~~ | careful | easy | initial | necessary | regular |
| smooth | successful | | | | |

Management at Dartington Crystal, a glass-producing company, decided to try an experiment to see if their workers could learn to work more [1] _efficiently_ . Many of their staff [2] _____ work a 50-hour week, but for the experiment, they agreed to keep to 40 hours. [3] _____ , everyone was very optimistic, but they found that they couldn't change their habits [4] _____ . They received training from a consultant who helped them to plan each day's work [5] _____ and to deal with the most important tasks first. After a few problems, the experiment ended [6] _____ : everyone worked shorter hours and the business continued to run [7] _____ . 'Working longer hours doesn't [8] _____ improve productivity,' the Managing Director said.

2 Put the adverb in the correct position a, b or c in each sentence.

1 We use software **a** to update **b** the information **c**.   (automatically)
2 Employees **a** have to **b** work **c** at night.   (sometimes)
3 All our sales staff **a** speak **b** English **c**.   (well)
4 We **a** send **b** orders **c** to suppliers every few hours.   (usually)
5 When we receive an order, we **a** have to **b** respond **c**.   (fast)
6 We check to make sure that everything **a** is **b** working **c**.   (efficiently)

3 Correct the mistakes in the checklist. There is one mistake in each sentence.

I plan exact what I have to do each day.

→ I plan _exactly_ what I have to do each day.

DO YOU
work efficiently?

1	I don't waste time doing things that aren't necessarily.	☐
2	I deal with importantly tasks immediately.	☐
3	I fill my time constructive.	☐
4	I skim read texts quick before I decide to read them in detail.	☐
5	My work area is always tidily.	☐
6	I share usefully ideas with friends or colleagues.	☐
7	I regular review my way of working.	☐
8	I try to find more efficiently ways of doing things.	☐
9	I only work a certainly number of hours every day.	☐

Work in pairs. Discuss the checklist above. Tell your partner what you usually do in order to be more efficient in your studies or in any job you do. What else could you do to improve your efficiency?

Managing time

There are many work situations where there is a time limit. In more formal meetings, it is usually the leader who makes sure that the meeting finishes on time. In informal meetings or team activities, any member of the group may remind the others about time.

The following expressions are useful for managing time:

a   *We don't have much time.*

b   *We must finish by 11 o'clock.*

c   *We're running out of time.*

d   *We need to be quick.*

e   *Could we quickly talk about ... ?*

f   *Can you please keep it short?*

g   *OK – it's time to finish.*

Listening 3

1 Listen to three extracts from a meeting, one from the start, one from the middle and one from the end of the meeting. Write *start, middle, end* below.

Extract 1 _____

Extract 2 _____

Extract 3 _____

2 Listen again and tick the phrases that you hear.

Speaking   Work in groups of 4–6. Your group has regular meetings where time is often wasted because everyone talks too much. Discuss how to make your meetings more efficient. Try to agree on five different ideas. Your teacher will give you a time limit for this discussion.

Culture at work

Managing time

When preparing meetings or organising your work, do you prepare a schedule and keep strictly to it? Or do you think it is better not to worry about a schedule, just use as much time as you need? Some cultures think of time as a precious resource that must be managed efficiently and not wasted. Others have a more flexible view of time. Which culture do you belong to?

Dilemma & Decision

Dilemma: Bonus or bust?

Brief

Scrutons Ltd is a small engineering firm that manufactures machine parts. The directors have a problem: productivity has fallen significantly in the last two years, and the business has started to suffer. The workers are failing to meet their production targets and the company is often late with deliveries to customers. There are also complaints about poor quality. The workers are unhappy because they are never able to earn their productivity bonuses. Morale is low. The situation has now reached a crisis: the company's reputation is badly damaged, sales are falling and financial losses amount to thousands of euros each month. What should the directors do?

Task 1

Read the background to the problem and the different options below. Prepare arguments for one of the four options.

Background to the problem

Two years ago, there was a disagreement between Patrick Massey (then the Production Manager) and the board of directors. Patrick wanted to give the workers an increase in pay, but the directors refused. They decided to introduce productivity bonuses instead. Following the disagreement, Patrick left the company. He was 58 and decided to take early retirement. Roland Court became the new Production Manager, but he is not a strong manager and is not popular with the workers.

Options:

1 Give a pay increase to all the workers (this would cost €500,000).
2 Reduce the level at which workers can earn a productivity bonus (this would cost €300,000).
3 Appoint a new production manager.
4 Cut labour costs (e.g. by not recruiting any new workers when people leave).

Task 2

Work in groups of 4–7. You represent the directors of Scrutons. Hold a meeting to decide what to do. Choose one person to lead the meeting. This person should start the discussion, ask people for their opinions, keep to the time limit and close the meeting.

Write it up

Write a memo to all the staff of Scrutons Ltd. Explain what you have decided to do.

Decision:

◉ Listen to George Mann, the Managing Director of Scrutons Ltd, talking about the decision which the directors took and what happened as a result.

Useful phrases

OK. Let's start. We have to decide …

What do you think?

Can you please keep it short?

Does anyone have any other opinions?

So can we agree to … ?

OK, it's time to finish.

Unit 14
Creativity

www.longman-elt.com   www.economist.com

How to be a brilliant thinker

Keynotes

We say that people are **creative** when they have new ideas that **challenge** the **traditional** ways of thinking. Creative people have **innovative** ideas for new products, and find **imaginative** ways to sell. But creativity is important in every field of business because creative **thinking** helps to solve problems. If you try to look at a problem from a different **perspective**, it may help you to find a **radical** solution.

Creative solutions

1 In small groups, study the two problems below. What do you think the solutions were?

Aquavision – aquarium manufacturer

Aquavision makes aquariums for the corporate market. It delivers the glass tank, equipment and fish, and installs the aquarium on site. It had a problem: the glass was often broken during transport. This cost the company a lot of money and caused delays for customers. The staff discussed several solutions. Could they find a new material instead of glass for the tanks? Could they improve the packaging? But none of these ideas gave them a satisfactory solution to the problem. What did they do?

Kinko's copy shops

Kinko's is a chain of shops offering photocopying facilities, including colour copying. Their problem was that business dropped significantly every December. This was because people were too busy preparing for Christmas to do much photocopying. What did they do to increase revenue at this time?

2 Turn to page 146 and read the solutions.

1 Read the article on the opposite page. What does the writer say we should do if we want to be brilliant thinkers? Tick all the correct answers.

1 study problems from a single perspective
2 look at problems from new directions
3 use traditional methods
4 consider a number of different perspectives
5 take time to study a problem

2 Complete the article with sentences a–e.

a You could study a satellite photo or a map.
b Competition in our business is not about price wars and money-off coupons.
c In this way, she was able to maximise revenue from the performances.
d They took an entirely different view and transformed society.
e How can we take a different view of a situation?

A different perspective

A wood might look like a random group of trees, but if you take a few steps to the side, you can see that all the trees are in rows. Sometimes we are standing in the wrong place to see an obvious answer. We have to deliberately take a different point of view before we have a chance of creating a radical solution. [1]____ Instead of looking at the scene from your view, try looking at it from the perspective of a customer, a child, an artist, a martian and so on.

What would you do if you had to study a river valley? You could look up and down the valley, you could look at it from the riverside or from each hillside. You could take a boat down the river. [2]____ Each gives you a different view of the valley. Why not do the same with a business problem?

Karen Brady became the Managing Director of Birmingham City football club at the age of 23. It was making huge losses but over the following ten years she transformed it into a thriving and profitable club. Her success is largely because she took a different point of view from the men who traditionally run the game. She saw the club as an events company. She applied new marketing methods to fill seats and sell affinity products, such as insurance, to the fans. [3]____

Lindsay Owen-Jones brought a new perspective when he became CEO of the French group L'Oréal, and has achieved remarkable growth. L'Oréal has a different point of view from consumer goods companies such as Unilever, which also sell cosmetics. Owen-Jones explains: [4]____ The consumer is guided by product performance. Is it pleasurable, imaginative and beautiful? Is this what I want at this moment in time?

The great innovators did not take the traditional view and develop existing ideas. [5]____ If we look at problems from new directions then we have unlimited possibilities for innovation.

Glossary

martian creature from the planet Mars

affinity products when these products are sold, some of the profit goes to the club

---

Speaking

1 Who would you consider to be 'a great innovator'?

2 Look at your classroom or your workplace from the perspective of an artist, a child or a martian. What would they notice?

Vocabulary 1 **Choose the best word or phrase in *italics* to replace the words in bold.**

1 The wood was a group of trees growing **in a random way**. *planned / unplanned*

2 The solution isn't always **obvious**. *hard to find / clear*

3 He broke the window **deliberately**. *accidentally / because he wanted to*

4 She **transformed** the company. *moved / changed*

5 She created a **thriving** club. *successful / popular*

Vocabulary 2 ## Multi-part verbs

1 *Look* can have different meanings when combined with different words. Match the verbs 1–5 with the meanings a–e.

1	look at	a	try to find something you have lost
2	look for	b	seem, or be similar to
3	look after	c	observe
4	look like	d	take care of, be responsible for
5	look forward to	e	be pleased about something that is going to happen

2 Complete the text with the correct forms of verbs from above.

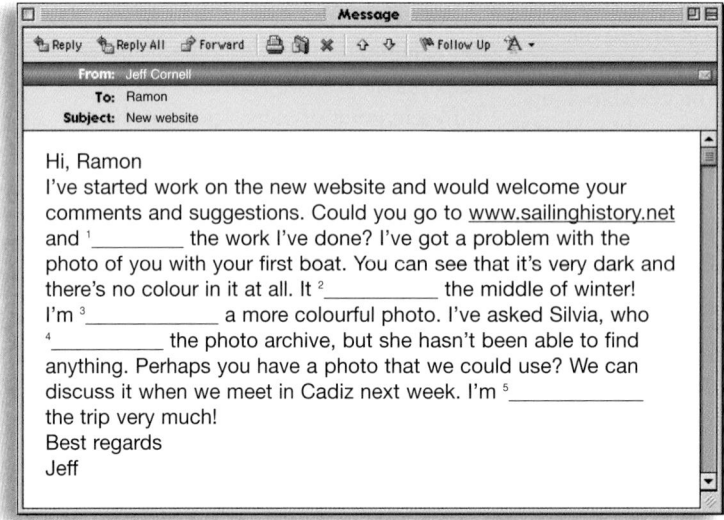

Message

Reply Reply All Forward ✉ ✕ ⇧ ⇩ Follow Up A ▾

From: Jeff Cornell
To: Ramon
Subject: New website

Hi, Ramon
I've started work on the new website and would welcome your comments and suggestions. Could you go to www.sailinghistory.net and ¹_____ the work I've done? I've got a problem with the photo of you with your first boat. You can see that it's very dark and there's no colour in it at all. It ²_____ the middle of winter! I'm ³_____ a more colourful photo. I've asked Silvia, who ⁴_____ the photo archive, but she hasn't been able to find anything. Perhaps you have a photo that we could use? We can discuss it when we meet in Cadiz next week. I'm ⁵_____ the trip very much!
Best regards
Jeff

Vocabulary 3 ## Suffixes

Look at these adjectives from the text and notice how they are formed from nouns.

tradition → tradition**al**   imagination → imaginat**ive**

profit → profit**able**   beauty → beaut**iful**

How do you form adjectives from the following nouns? Use a dictionary.

1 practice 2 success 3 competition 4 accident

5 innovation 6 care 7 reason 8 fashion

Pronunciation ⊙ Listen to the pronunciation of some of the nouns and adjectives. Write the words you hear and mark the stress.

e*co*nomy   eco*no*mical

noun	adjective
1 _____	_____
2 _____	_____
3 _____	_____
4 _____	_____

Listening 1 ⊙

Developing company creativity

1 Paul Saunders, a consultant, talks about the importance of developing creativity. Listen to part one and answer the questions.

1 In what fields of business is creativity especially important?
2 Why is it so important for companies to do something different?

2 Listen to part two and complete the sentences.

1 Adaptors are _____ . They look after the_____ .
2 They are important for _____ in the day-to-day running of the business.
3 Innovators are people who want _____ . They like to challenge the normal way of doing things and are happy to _____ .
4 They are important to a company when _____ .
5 It's essential for managers to encourage their staff to _____ and be ready to try new things.
6 To be a creative leader, you have to _____ .

Language check

Conditional 2

Study the examples and complete the rules below.

– What **would** you do if you **had** to study a river valley?
– If you **went** up in a spaceship, you **would** see the world differently.
– It **would** be easier if we **discussed** the problem together.
– People **would** suggest more new ideas if they **weren't** afraid of criticism.
– Most people **could** be more creative if they **practised** a few exercises.
– If we **had** more money, we **could** invest in research.

1 In conditional 2, the verb following *if* is in the _____ tense.
2 The verb in the other half of the sentence is formed with _____ or _____ , plus the infinitive.
3 What is the difference in meaning between these sentences?
   If you take a boat, you'll see more. / If you took a boat, you'd see more.
4 Which one of the following is not correct?
   We use conditional 2 to ...

   ☐ talk about the future result of a possible action.
   ☐ imagine the result of improbable or unreal situations.

For more information, see page 160.

1 **Choose the correct form of the verbs in *italics*.**

1 If I think of any new ideas, *I'll / I'd* phone you.

2 If we had more time, we *can / could* do more careful research.

3 People would be more creative if they *weren't / wouldn't be* so stressed.

4 If we *have / had* a more exciting product, we'd sell more.

5 People will buy the product if we *make / made* it more exciting.

6 *Will / Would* companies be more innovative if they encouraged more discussion?

7 If we *don't / didn't* take risks sometimes, we would never make any progress.

8 What would we do if the venture *failed / would fail*?

2 **Write a sentence about each person's wish using the second conditional.**

Pascale works in an open-plan office with a lot of other people. The office is noisy and it's difficult to work. He'd like to have his own office.

'If I had my own office, it would be easier to work.'

1 Marta has young children at school but also works full-time. She has to work fixed hours from 9am to 5pm. She'd like to work flexi-time so she can meet her children from school.

'If I ...'

2 Don travels a lot in his work. He has a young family but he doesn't see them very often. He would like to travel less and spend more time with his family.

'If I ...'

3 Trudy has to travel for an hour by train every day to get to work. It is tiring and expensive. She would like to work from home for part of the week, to save time and costs.

'If I ...'

4 Felipe has a tough boss who expects him to work very long hours. He feels very stressed. He'd like to have a more sympathetic boss.

'If I ...'

What would make *your* life easier? Work in small groups. Tell the others what you would like to change and why. Use conditional 2.

Finding creative solutions

When your company or your team faces a difficult situation, you need to look for a creative solution. It is a good idea to meet and brainstorm as many possible solutions as you can and make a list. Don't discuss the ideas yet. Don't reject any of them. Write down all the ideas, even crazy ones. When you have a list, you can evaluate the ideas to see which ones would (or wouldn't) work. It helps if you make a statement about what kind of solution you really want.

Look at the following examples. Which ones are useful for brainstorming? Which ones are useful for evaluating? Which one helps you to define the solution you want?

Would it help if ... ?

If we did that, it would be ...

What else could we do?

That could be a solution.

What if we ... ?

That wouldn't work / wouldn't help.

What we really want is ...

Problem

A large finance company has just produced an expensive colour brochure. Two million copies have been printed. Unfortunately, there is a mistake. The telephone number for customer enquiries is written as 0050 040 050. The number should be: 0050 040 040.

Listening 2 ⊙

1 Listen to three members of the company's marketing department evaluating the three possible solutions below. Which ones would / wouldn't work? Why? / Why not?

- reprint all the brochures
- fire the person responsible
- print labels with the correct number and stick them on

2 Listen to the next part of the discussion. Someone suggests a new idea. What is it? Could it work?

Speaking

You are the managers of a small company. Your staff are using too much paper. It is a high cost and much of it is wasted. How can you encourage people to use less paper? Brainstorm as many ideas as you can and make a list. Then evaluate the ideas and decide which one(s) would work best.

Culture at work

Showing disagreement

If you disagree with someone in a meeting, do you say: 'I disagree completely!' or 'Yes, I see what you mean, but ...'? In some cultures, people think it is normal to express disagreement directly. In other cultures, people find this too aggressive. They never say 'I disagree!' Instead, they politely suggest another way of looking at the problem. Which kind of culture do you belong to?

Dilemma & Decision

Dilemma: Gold rush

Brief

Goldcorp is a company that mines gold in Canada. The company owns the Red Lake mine, which is not productive.

goldcorp inc.

In 50 years of production, only 3 million ounces have been extracted and the quality of this gold is low grade. The mine's costs are high and the company is losing money fast. Rob McEwen, the CEO, believes there is more gold on the site. Other mines in the area have produced high quality gold: one mine has produced more than 10 million ounces. Perhaps this source of gold also runs into the Red Lake site. If the company could make a new discovery, all their problems would be solved! But exploration is slow. The small team of geologists working on the problem has a lot of work to do to analyse all the data, and the gold lies at more than 1,000 metres below the ground, so testing is expensive. What could the company do?

Here are some possible solutions:

1. Close the mine and cut losses.
2. Invest in more geologists and new equipment and try to speed up the exploration.
3. Continue to explore with the existing team and no new investment.
4. Hold a competition to find the gold.
5. Another solution?

Task

In small groups, hold a meeting to evaluate each of the above solutions. Can you think of any other ideas? Try brainstorming some more creative solutions.

Write it up

Write a summary of your meeting. List each of the solutions that you discussed, and outline what you think could or would happen if you took this action.

Decision:

⊙ Now listen to a financial news report about Goldcorp.

Useful phrases

What would happen if we ... ?
We'd be able to ...
If we did that, it would be ...
What else could we do?
That wouldn't work / wouldn't help.

Unit 15
Motivation

www.longman-elt.com   www.economist.com

Having fun at work

Keynotes

People work hard because they are motivated to **achieve** something. Many companies **encourage** hard work by offering higher **pay** and **bonuses** for good **performance**. In the past, companies **rewarded** long-term service and **loyalty** to the company. Staff were motivated by the chance of **promotion** to **senior** positions. Nowadays, companies are less **hierarchical**, and people change jobs more often. This means that companies have to find new ways to attract and keep **talented** workers – for example by creating a more exciting working environment.

What motivates you to work harder?

Choose three factors from the list. Explain your choices to a partner.

1 the prospect of earning good money in the future
2 competition with others
3 working in a friendly environment
4 having fun while you work
5 receiving praise
6 meeting a challenge
7 working on something that is interesting and exciting
8 feeling confident that you can do something well

1 **Listen to Dilys Breeze, a human resources manager, talking about motivating workers in her company. Which of the factors in the list above does she mention?**

2 **Listen again and complete the text.**

Most people feel motivated when they know they are making a
¹_____ and doing something ²_____ .
People need to receive praise. They want to feel that others
³_____ their problems or suggestions. And most want to
develop their ⁴_____ and ⁵_____ new things.

3 **Tick what managers should do, according to Dilys Breeze.**

stimulate ☐   encourage ☐   criticise ☐   support ☐
listen ☐   shout ☐   help ☐   instruct ☐

Did you have similar ideas to Dilys Breeze?

1 **Read the article on the opposite page and find four reasons why some companies are trying to attract young workers.**

2 **Read the article again and answer the following questions.**

1 What does CapitalOne offer its employees?
2 What five things are most important to young people in their work?

3 **Which of the following things were generally true in the past (P) and which are true today (T), according to the article?**

1 Office culture is formal.
2 People only become top managers after years of loyal service.
3 Companies can grow rapidly and also fail suddenly.
4 Workers have to show respect for their superiors.
5 Companies prefer workers who understand e-business.
6 People work for the same company all their lives.
7 Young people have many opportunities to show creativity.

Survey: The young

The kids are all right

Young people at work can now expect opportunity, responsibility, respect – and fun

1 Youth is a time for fun. In one American playground in Florida, there are basketball courts and volleyball nets. Inside, there are bright colours, Nerf guns and a games room with pingpong. This is not a school, but the offices of CapitalOne, one of America's largest credit-card firms. The firm gives each department a monthly "fun budget". The same sort of thing can be found across corporate America these days. The kids have taken over. It is technology that drives business today, and dot.com culture is everywhere. The young are now the rising power in the workplace.

2 Take Microsoft, a business with 40,000 mostly young employees: the dress code is "anything goes as long as you're clean". People wear shorts and have blue hair – sometimes even in management. The typical workplace scene features mid-afternoon hockey, video games and techno music on headphones.

3 Companies want to attract and keep a younger workforce because of its technical skills and enthusiasm for change. So youth culture is becoming part of office culture. This may be no bad thing. Along with the company fun budget come things that matter more deeply to young people: opportunity, responsibility, respect.

4 In the past, it was the middle-aged who ruled. At work, grey hair, years of loyal service and seniority counted most. Now things are changing. Older workers will not disappear, but they will have to share power with the young. In the old days companies grew slowly; with success came conservative corporate values. Now the world's largest firms can crash at any moment. The pace of change is increasing. And change favours the young: they learn and relearn faster and will risk more to try new things.

5 Many companies no longer have seniority-based hierarchies. People can get to the top faster. They don't have to spend years showing respect for their superiors. It is more important that they are able to understand e-business and have the courage to ask "why?". Loyalty to the company is less important than talent. Employees stay only when there are challenges and rewards. Changing jobs frequently is now a sign of ambition and initiative.

6 All this is a good thing. Young people are at their most creative stage in life. Now they have more opportunity to put their ideas and energy into practice. ∎

Glossary

Nerf guns realistic toy guns that shoot but don't cause injuries

Speaking

1 Would you like to work for CapitalOne or Microsoft? Why? / Why not?

2 In what ways is the office culture in companies in your country similar to or different from the culture of CapitalOne or Microsoft?

Personal qualities

Find the words in the article that match these personal qualities.

1 a strong feeling of interest and excitement about something:
 e_____ (paragraph 3)

2 the ability to be brave enough to do or say something you think is right:
 c_____ (paragraph 5)

3 staying faithful to one company: l_____ (paragraph 5)

4 a special natural ability or skill: t_____ (paragraph 5)

5 determination to be successful, to achieve something: a_____
 (paragraph 5)

6 the ability to do something without waiting to be told what to do:
 i_____ (paragraph 5)

Management styles

Complete the text with the following words.

| hierarchy | level | reward | senior | superiors | subordinates |
| responsibility | seniority | | | | |

Some companies have a complex ¹_____ with many levels of
management; ²_____ managers are very powerful, so it is important
to show them great respect and ³_____ are generally afraid to question
the decisions of their ⁴_____ . Other companies are less hierarchical.
People respect each other because of their skills, not because of their
⁵_____ . These companies give younger employees more ⁶_____ .
They ⁷_____ good ideas from every ⁸_____ in the organisation.

Multi-part verbs

1 *Take* **can have different meanings when combined with different
words. Study the examples and match the verbs a–f with their
meanings 1–6.**

1 The kids have **taken over**.

2 The company has **taken on** 20 new staff.

3 Maria has **taken up** the job offer from Microsoft.

4 The management told John to **take off** his earrings at work.

5 Everyone in the department **took part** in the volleyball match.

6 The meeting will **take place** on Monday at 09:00.

a remove

b take control of something

c recruit or hire

d accept

e happen

f do an activity, participate

2 Complete the sentences with the following words.

on	off	up	over	part	place

1 The company was reorganised after John Green took _____ as CEO.
2 We offered the staff a bonus in exchange for a reduction of holiday time, but they didn't take it _____ .
3 When it's hot, the men often take _____ their jackets and ties.
4 All the staff we've taken _____ this year are under 25.
5 Would you like to take _____ in the company quiz night?
6 The final match will take _____ on Friday at 4pm.

Language check # Present perfect and past simple

Match the examples 1–6 with the rules a–e. One of the rules matches two examples.

1 In the old days, companies **grew** slowly.
2 Now the kids **have taken over.**
3 Jack Welch **took over** as CEO of GE in 1981.
4 He **was** CEO for 20 years, and retired in 2001.
5 Mike works for MV. He **has been** with the company for three years now.
6 Mike **has worked** at head office since June.

a We use the past simple to talk about things that belong to the past and are finished.
b We use the past simple when we give the specific time that an event took place.
c We use the present perfect to show the result of an event without saying when it happened.
d We use the present perfect with *for* and *since* to talk about things that started in the past but continue up to the present.
e We use the past simple with *for* when the activity is finished.

 For more information, see pages 159 and 160.

Practice **1** Choose the best explanation, a or b, for each sentence.

1 Profits continued to fall for several years.
   a profits are still falling
   b profits fell in the past, but now the situation has changed
2 Recent job cuts have caused staff to feel demotivated.
   a staff are now feeling demotivated
   b staff felt demotivated in the past, but now they feel differently
3 The company has stayed ahead of its competitors for seven years.
   a it is still ahead of its competitors
   b it is no longer ahead of its competitors
4 Jean Deneuve has been a member of the design team since 2001.
   a Jean is still a member of the design team
   b Jean is no longer a member of the design team

2 Complete the text with the present perfect or past simple form of the verbs in brackets.

Christian Rufer is an accountant with Taurus, a finance company. He (¹work) _____ for the company for ten years. Since he first started, there (²be) _____ many changes. 'For many years,' he says, 'the company (³have) _____ a rigid hierarchy with many levels of management. Then Gerhard Brock (⁴take over) _____ as CEO two years ago. Brock's first decision was to re-structure the company to create a flatter hierarchy. Since then, a completely new management style (⁵develop) _____ . In the past, staff (⁶come) _____ to work at 8:00 every morning. Now the company (⁷change) _____ to flexible working hours and staff can start and finish when they want. In the old days, staff (⁸receive) _____ fixed salaries based on their seniority. But now, staff are able to earn bonuses based on performance and productivity. In the last two years, I (⁹enjoy) _____ my job much more. I think it's great!'

Speaking

Tell your partner about something that has changed in your personal life, in your work or in your country in the last year or two. Explain how things were in the past and what has happened since the change.

Listening 2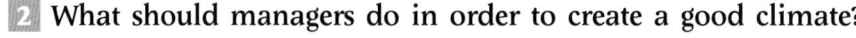

What workers need in order to feel motivated

1 Listen to Clark Morris, a human resources consultant, talking about four factors that contribute to employee motivation. Match the factors 1–4 with the explanations a–d.

1	connection	a	We need to enjoy our job and get satisfaction from it.
2	content	b	Staff need to have a good relationship with managers.
3	context	c	We need to understand our role in the company.
4	climate	d	The company's systems need to work well.

2 What should managers do in order to create a good climate?

Giving reasons

In business you often have to change things. The reasons for your decision may not be clear to others, and then you have to give an explanation. The following phrases are useful for giving reasons and explanations.

so that (we can ...)

so ... (in the middle of a sentence)

That means that ... (at the start of a sentence)

because ... (+ verb phrase)

because of (+ noun)

in order to ... (+ infinitive)

Listening 3

1 Listen to five extracts from job interviews. Answer the questions.

1 Why did Terry leave his previous job?

2 Why did Tanya leave her previous job?

3 Why did Tanya apply for this job?

4 Why did Tim decide to change his job?

5 Why did Tim apply for this job?

2 Listen again. Which of the above phrases did you hear?

3 Complete the sentences using the phrases above.

1 We introduced a new system _____ the old one wasn't efficient.

2 Your team has achieved excellent results, _____ we've decided to give you all a bonus.

3 Too many people are arriving late for work. _____ there aren't enough staff on duty early in the morning.

4 We have decided to start a gym club in the company _____ staff can keep fit.

5 _____ our weak position, we can't increase salaries.

6 _____ celebrate our 100th anniversary, the directors have decided to give all staff an extra day's holiday.

Speaking

Set yourself three goals for the coming year (e.g. continue to improve English, get a new job, get fit, etc.). Tell your partner about them and explain why you want to do them. Use the language above.

Culture at work

Formal and informal presentations

Do you think business presentations should be formal or informal? In formal presentations, the speaker usually wears smart clothes and uses very polite language. They don't make much direct contact with the audience. In informal presentations, speakers wear casual clothes and use more everyday language. They talk in a friendly way to the audience, often asking questions and accepting interruptions. Some cultures prefer business presentations to be formal; others prefer a more informal style. Which culture do you belong to?

Dilemma & Decision

Dilemma: Hot-desking

Brief

You are the senior managers of Sirius, a company selling network solutions B2B. You employ 115 staff: 40 sales consultants, 50 technical staff (programmers, software designers) and 25 administrative staff (accountants, lawyers, etc.). Because of a recent downturn in your business, together with the rising cost of office rent, you now have to move to a smaller office. This means that each member of staff will have less work space. However, the sales staff are out of the office for much of the time. Should you introduce hot-desking or give each worker an individual work space? There are good reasons for introducing hot-desking, but it seems that many of the staff are against the idea.

Hot-desking

Workers do not have their own desks. They choose a different space to work in each day. They each have laptop computers and mobile phones, and there are cupboards where they can store their files, books and personal items. Workers can choose to work in team rooms or quiet rooms. Only the senior managers have individual offices.

Individual work spaces

The office space is divided into small units: each person has their own space with a desk and PC, surrounded by a screen. Managers and senior staff have bigger offices with walls, windows and a door. There are meeting rooms where teams can get together.

Task 1

You are going to find out what different staff members think. Work in two groups. Group A turn to page 140. Group B turn to page 144.

Task 2

Form new groups with students from group A and group B. Present your decision to the others and explain your reasons. When you listen to the other group's decision, ask for explanations if necessary.

Write it up

Write a memo to the staff telling them what decision you have taken and why.

Decision:

⊙ Now listen to Kok Tan Hiang, the CEO of a Hong Kong software design company, explaining the decision that was taken when his company moved to new offices.

Useful phrases

We've decided to / not to …

We think this is the best solution because …

This means that …

So that …

In order to …

Review 5

Language check

Choose the correct form of the words in *italics*.

A study was [1]*recent / recently* carried out into the productivity of 160 engineers. The engineers worked in teams but also did many tasks [2]*individual / individually*. The study looked at how [3]*frequent / frequently* the engineers helped each other. Engineers were also asked to say how [4]*high / highly* they respected each of their colleagues. The study found that [5]*helpful / helpfully* engineers received a [6]*high / highly* level of respect from their colleagues. However, if they gave help but didn't receive much, they were not very [7]*productive / productively*. Those engineers who accepted help as well as giving it were able to boost their productivity and were also more [8]*popular/ popularly* with their colleagues.

Conditional 2

Complete the sentences with the correct form of the verbs in brackets.

1 If the staff (be) _____ more motivated, they would be more productive.

2 People (not look) _____ for new jobs if their pay was higher.

3 Henry would stay in the same company if he (have) _____ better career opportunities.

4 It would be difficult to attract new staff if we (not offer) _____ good salaries.

5 I (enjoy) _____ my job more if I could be more creative.

6 Susan doesn't like working alone. She'd be happier if she (be) _____ part of a team.

7 The staff (work) _____ more efficiently if their office was more up-to-date.

8 If we (install) _____ a new computer system, we could do the work in half the time.

Present perfect and past simple

Complete the text with the present perfect or past simple of the verbs in brackets.

Peter Grossman ([1]start) _____ his career as an insurance clerk in 1997. But after four years, he ([2]leave) _____ this job, and ([3]join) _____

Hertleins, a financial services company. He ([4]be) _____ with this company since 2001. Since joining Hertleins, he ([5]have) _____ two different kinds of job. To begin with, he ([6]sell) _____ investments to customers all over the country. But he ([7]not like) _____ selling very much, so he ([8]ask) _____ the company if he could move to another department. Now he works as an assistant in the Human Resources department. He ([9]work) _____ in this job for nearly two years now.

Choose the correct form of the word or phrase in *italics*.

In the past, Britons mainly [1]*drank / have drunk* tea; but in recent years, coffee [2]*became / has become* increasingly popular. Chains of coffee shops, such as Starbucks, [3]*opened / have opened* in city centres across the country and now more than 80 per cent of Britons visit a coffee shop at least once a week. Spending on coffee [4]*rose / has risen* by 15 per cent since last year. A [5]*recent / recently* report shows that Starbucks is the chain that is growing most [6]*rapid / rapidly* and has a market share of 25 per cent. Costa Coffee is a [7]*close / closely* competitor with a 21 per cent market share. The number of coffee shops in city centres [8]*now reached / has now reached* a maximum level, and the chains are trying to expand into small towns. This could be bad news for small cafés: if the chains continue to expand, many small outlets [9]*would / could* go out of business.

We asked two consumers for their opinions on coffee shops. Matt Wingford, an accountant, says: 'I like the coffee – it's excellent. But my local coffee shop is often very [10]*noisy / noisily*. I [11]*went / would go* more often if it [12]*would be / was* quieter.' Cathy Mansfield, a student, says: 'It's great. My friends and I go there [13]*regular / regularly*. But the coffee is quite expensive. I [14]*will / would* drink more coffee if it [15]*is / was* cheaper.'

Vocabulary check

Choose the best option, a–c to complete the text.

The product development team at Playtime plc, a toy ¹_____ , were highly ²_____ . They produced a ³_____ number of good ideas for new toys, which meant that their company was able to extend its ⁴_____ of popular products. But things changed when the team's manager left to join a competitor. The new manager was much less successful in ⁵_____ the team. Instead of ⁶_____ staff and praising them for their ideas, he put pressure on them. He tried to make them work harder and longer. This didn't increase their ⁷_____ : it reduced it. In fact, as the team became more and more stressed, their ⁸_____ declined. Their product ideas were unpopular and failed to satisfy customer ⁹_____ . Now the company is losing market share and needs to find a ¹⁰_____ solution.

1. a manufacturing
   b manufacturer
   c manufacture
2. a innovative
   b imagining
   c thinking
3. a short
   b remarkable
   c important
4. a quantity
   b amount
   c range
5. a making
   b motivating
   c supplying
6. a encouraging
   b improving
   c contributing
7. a efficiency
   b production
   c process
8. a creative
   b creativity
   c creation
9. a delay
   b discovery
   c demand
10. a real
    b radical
    c traditional

Career skills

Choose a phrase from the list a–h to complete the reminders about time.

1. We don't have ...
2. We must finish ...
3. It's time ...
4. We're running ...
5. Please keep it ...

a by 5 o'clock.
b out of time.
c quick.
d much time.
e to 12:30.
f with delay.
g short.
h to finish.

Finding creative solutions

Complete the dialogue with the following phrases.

Would it help if   That could be a solution
If we did that   What could we do   What if we
That wouldn't help

A The sales staff are selling lots of products, but it takes us too long to deliver the orders to the customer. ¹_____ to make the system more efficient?

B ²_____ took on more sales staff?

A ³_____ . We've got enough staff. It's the order processing system that's not working well.

C ⁴_____ the sales reps carried laptops when they visited the customers? That way, they could enter orders immediately.

B Yes! ⁵_____ , we could reduce the time it takes to transfer orders to the sales office.

A ⁶_____ !

Giving reasons

Complete the reasons with the following phrases.

because   because of   so that   in order
means that

1. I need a large desk _____ I have a lot of books and papers.
2. You should make lists of things to do _____ you don't forget anything.
3. A lot of people have to work in a quiet environment _____ to think clearly.
4. I usually switch off my mobile phone when I'm working. This _____ I don't get any interruptions.
5. I can't work at home _____ the television.

Pairwork

Unit 1   page 14 **Dilemma Group A:** George Johnstone

- An excellent salesman. Has good relations with the customers in the US and Canada.
- 32 years old and single. Keen to expand his area of responsibility.
- Travels a lot on business. Mexico easy because close to US.
- Doesn't speak Spanish and no experience in Spanish-speaking cultures.

Unit 2   page 22 **Dilemma Group A**

Read the answers to questions 1, 3, 5, 7.

1   18 million people have internet access (2005). Expected to double in 2 to 3 years.
3   Teenagers and students are the biggest groups of users.
5   Telephone lines are bad. Problems connecting to the internet, and it is very slow.
7   Largest online retailer is Baazee, online auction company, with 1 million users.

Unit 3   page 28 **Student A**

Role-play situations. Ask Student B for help. Offer to help if you can.

1   You want to phone a colleague, but you don't have his/her telephone number.
2   You want to print out a report but your printer isn't working.
3   Your train leaves in 10 minutes. It is a 20-minute-walk to the station. Student B has a car.

Unit 4   page 39 **Student A**

This CD rack stores 180 CDs. It is made of metal. Who do you think are the target customers? Do you like this product or not? Describe the product to Student B.

Now listen to Student B's product description and complete the chart.

Product	
Use(s)	
Features	
Looks	
Target customers	

Unit 5   page 48 **Dilemma Group A**

Read about Rocky Farm. What do you think are its strengths and weaknesses?

2000   Ken and Patsy Carr produce organic ice cream.

2002   They start selling ice cream to local hotels and restaurants.

2003   They increase production and staff.

2004   They win a prize for the most delicious ice cream in the country.

Current situation

Very profitable business. Low production costs. But difficult to meet increasing demand. Ken and Patsy want a bigger factory, but will have to borrow a lot of money.

Unit 6   page 56 **Dilemma Group A**

Read the information about Celf Cure. Make notes about the technology and its future market potential.

Celf Cure

With Celf Cure, the body repairs itself. This company wants to introduce a new technique to treat people with common diseases such as heart disease. Doctors take cells from the sick person's body, treat the cells in a laboratory with drugs and then put them back into the body. Research shows that this is very effective. This is an existing company that has already had success with other medical products.

Unit 7   page 66 **Dilemma Group A**

Read about Luton. Which factors in the list in Task 1 does Luton provide? Make notes and prepare to present your ideas to the class.

General:	Luton is a manufacturing town with a population of 184,000.
Economy:	A growing economy with many businesses: cars, electronics, aircraft and airlines, travel companies, pharmaceuticals.
Infrastructure:	Close to M1 motorway. London 30 minutes by rail. Large airport.
Commercial premises:	There is a wide range of commercial premises available. There are plans to build a new business park and a technology village.

Unit 8   page 74 **Dilemma Group A: Wide World Tours**

Job title: Marketing Assistant, Marketing Department   Pay: €30,000 per year

Responsibilities: Maintain customer database, carry out market research, help with promotions. No travel opportunities.

The company: Large modern offices, restaurant and sports facilities.

Opportunities for training and development.

An existing employee says: 'You have to be ready to work very hard. Great opportunities for people with energy and ambition.'

Unit 9   page 82 Dilemma Group A: Standard job recruitment methods

Method: Post a job advertisement → Select from written applications → Hold interviews in each university

Points to discuss:

Decide where you could put the advertisement.

What could you put in the advertisement?

What could you offer students to encourage them to apply?

Unit 10   page 91 Student A

Petra is a student who works part-time in a café. Graph A shows the wages and tips she received last week. Describe the graph to Student B.

A
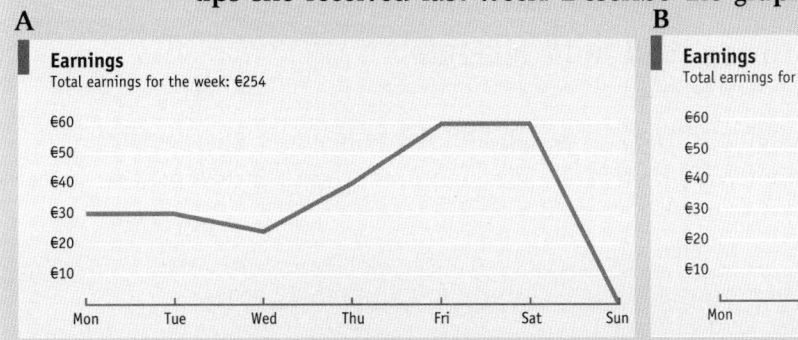

B
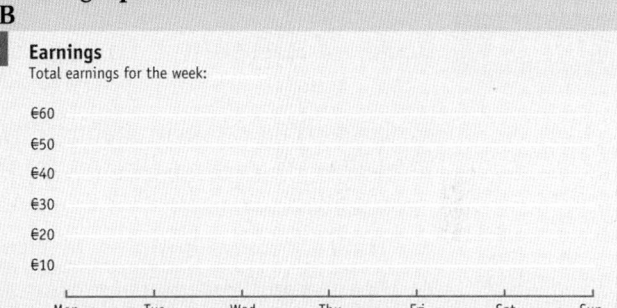

Toni is a music student who gives piano lessons at €20 per hour. Listen to Student B's description of Toni's wages last week and complete graph B.

Unit 11   page 100 Dilemma Group A: Insurance company

Read the arguments. Make notes and prepare for a meeting.

1 You will not pay a claim for theft of a vehicle except when all doors and windows are locked, the keys are removed and the security devices are set.

2 Your contract says: 'The insured person must take all reasonable steps to prevent loss or damage.' You think Jane Buxton didn't do this.

3 Jane knew that a thief had her address and car keys. It was obvious that she should replace the locks.

Unit 12   page 108 Dilemma Group A: Recruit more staff

Current situation

Many employees stay only a few months. It is difficult to replace people and there aren't enough staff in the stores.

Possible good results: More staff to help customers.

Possible bad results: Higher recruitment costs and higher salary costs.

Unit 15 page 134 **Dilemma Group A**

Read the opinions, discuss them and decide whether to introduce hot-desking or not. Make a list of the reasons.

Human Resources Manager

'It will create a more dynamic environment. Staff can communicate more easily. People will work next to different colleagues, so everyone will know everyone else.'

Young sales consultant

'I'm out of the office most of the time. I often work at home, or in my car. I only come to the office for team meetings so I don't need my own space.'

Accountant

'I like family photos on my desk and my personal things around me.'

Unit 1 page 14 **Dilemma Group B: Linda McCade**

- Linda is an excellent manager. She is very good at planning and organising her work.
- Speaks Spanish. Experience of Spanish-speaking cultures. Good relationships with Spanish customers.
- Travels a lot on business. Mexico would mean longer flights.
- 29 years old and married. Hopes to start a family in two to three years.

Unit 2 page 21 **Student B**

Write the information that Student A gives you.

Now give your partner this information.

Name: Harry Clarke Age: 28
Salary: $52,430 a year
Car: buys new car every year; expects to spend $50,000 on next car
Drives 30,800 kilometres a year
Works in a company with 8,940 employees
Spends 4.1% of salary on clothes

Unit 2 page 22 **Dilemma Group B**

Read the answers to questions 2, 4, 6.

2 Most people use internet cafés. Not many computers at home – expensive.

4 Most people use the internet for email (72%), or entertainment; 50% of young users use it for education and studying. Very few do internet shopping.

6 Not many people use credit cards. Online shoppers use cheque or bank.

page 28 **Student B**

Role-play situations. Ask Student A for help. Offer to help if you can.

1   You want to write a letter in English but you haven't got a dictionary.
2   You want to buy some chocolate from a machine but you haven't got any coins.
3   You have to give a presentation tomorrow about the economy of your country. You don't know much about it. Your partner is an expert on this subject.

Unit 3   page 30 **Dilemma Group A**

Some bullies love power. They want to be in control of everything and everybody. These bullies make life difficult for all their subordinates. They usually have psychological problems and it isn't easy to change their management style.

Unit 4   page 39 **Student B**

Listen to Student A's product description and complete the chart.

Product	
Use(s)	
Features	
Looks	
Target customers	

This bookcase stores 100 books. It is made of cheap but strong wood. Who do you think are the target customers? Do you like this product or not? Describe the product to Student A.

Unit 5   page 47 **Student B**

Ask and answer questions to find out the story of Jeff Bezos and Amazon and complete the chart.

Year	Event
1986	Graduated from Princeton
	First job – with a new technology company
1992	Became senior vice president of DE Shaw, a Wall St firm
1993	
1993	Moved to Seattle, began writing software for new business
	Amazon opened for business
1997	Amazon sales increased but it didn't make a profit
2000	

Unit 5 · page 48 Dilemma Group B

Read about Annie's Kitchen. What do you think are its strengths and weaknesses?

1996	Annie Ross produces organic yoghurt to sell to local shops and restaurants.
1998	Annie's yoghurts very popular – she decides to make ice cream as well.
1999	Sets up website and starts selling around the country. Employs 35 people.
2002	Moves production to a bigger factory. Number of staff increases to 80.
2004	Problems with the distributor. The company loses €40,000.

Current situation

Moving to a bigger factory was a high cost: Annie has to pay a lot of money to the bank. It is difficult to make enough money to meet all the costs. Following problems with the distributor, the firm now has big financial difficulties.

Unit 6 · page 56 Dilemma Group B

Read the information about Space Travel Inc. Make notes about the technology and its potential future market.

Space Travel Inc. is a new company that has developed a spacecraft for tourists looking for adventure. The spacecraft can carry six to eight people up into space at a cost of $30,000 each. The cost of maintenance and insurance will be high.

Unit 7 · page 66 Dilemma Group B

Read about Swindon. Which factors in the list in Task 1 does Swindon provide? Make notes and prepare to present your ideas to the class.

General:	Swindon is a famous railway town, in the past a manufacturing town with a population of 157,000.
Economy:	Many manufacturing companies closed and people lost jobs. New businesses setting up include: car manufacturing, mobile communications, transport.
Infrastructure:	Close to M4 motorway. Excellent rail communications. London one hour by rail. The nearest airport (one hour by road) is Heathrow, London's biggest airport.
Commercial premises:	Modern business parks with high quality office premises.

Unit 8 · page 74 Dilemma Group B: Oz Travel

Job title: Travel consultant   Pay: €22,000

Responsibilities: Deal with phone enquiries, sell tours, provide customer service; deal with suppliers by phone and email; general administration if necessary.

Travel: Visit Australia, help set up new contacts and new tours.

The company: Small office in city centre. Small business but if successful, may expand.

An existing employee says: 'It is a very friendly place to work, but it can be stressful.'

Unit 9 | page 82 **Dilemma Group B: Attend student fairs**

Universities hold fairs for students at the start of each year. Different companies have stands at these fairs to sell their products or services to students. Students can find out about things that may be helpful during their student life.

Method:

Set up a Virgin Mobile stand at student fairs.

Tell students who come to the stand about marketing opportunities.

Recruit interested students 'on the spot'.

Points to discuss:

Decide how to attract students' attention at the fair.

What could you do to encourage students to apply for the work?

How could you choose the most talented students during the short time available?

Unit 10 | page 91 **Student B**

Petra is a student who works part-time in a café. Listen to Student A's description of Petra's wages and tips last week and complete graph A.

A
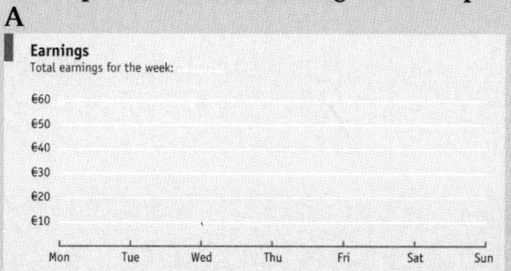

B
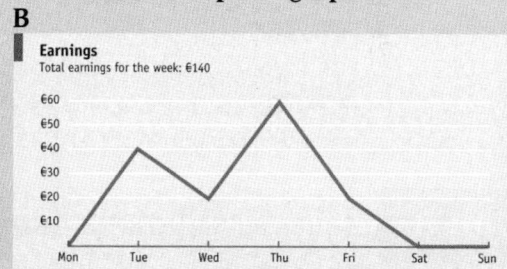

Toni is a music student who gives piano lessons at €20 per hour. Graph B shows the money he made last week. Describe the graph to Student A.

Unit 11 | page 100 **Dilemma Group B: Jane Buxton**

Read your arguments. Make notes and prepare for a meeting.

1 The car was old with a value of only €2,000. New locks would cost €1,000.
2 You reported the theft of your handbag to the police and also to your insurance company. But nobody told you to replace the car's locks after the keys were stolen.
3 You didn't know that you wouldn't be able to claim if your car was stolen.

Unit 3 | page 30 **Dilemma Group B**

Some bullies hate mistakes. They want their own work to be perfect and they want everyone else to be perfect too. These bullies don't consider other people's feelings when they find problems with their work. They often don't know they are bullying. Sometimes it can help to talk to these bullies about their management style.

Unit 12   page 108 Dilemma Group B: Improve training

Current situation

New staff receive one day's training then learn on the job. Many people stay only a few months. There aren't enough experienced workers.

Possible good results: Staff will learn about the products and how to deal with customers.

Possible bad results: High cost; trained staff may leave the company.

Unit 15   page 134 Dilemma Group B

Read the opinions, discuss them and decide whether to introduce hot-desking or not. Make a list of your reasons.

Office manager

'It needs to be well-organised. If people can't find space, they'll get demotivated.'

Young programmer

'It'll be fun. I like it. I won't have to work in the same place all the time.'

Lawyer

'I'll have to carry lots of heavy books around. I don't think hot-desking would work for me at all.'

Unit 3   page 30 Dilemma Group C

Some people become bullies because they are very unsure of themselves. They are afraid of competition from other people who may be better than them. They hate the idea of someone else doing well in their job. They think that the only way to improve their own success is to keep their competitors back.

Unit 5   page 48 Dilemma Group C

Read about Golden Valley. What do you think are its strengths and weaknesses?

1993   Six organic farmers start selling organic dairy products to local shops.

1995   They found the Golden Valley company and start to sell more products.

1997   Company distributes to shops and supermarkets around the country.

1998   Production moves to big new processing plant.

2000   Company becomes market leader (35 per cent of organic dairy food market).

Current situation

The company employs 200 staff. It has a large range of products, supplies most of the big supermarkets and is very profitable.

Unit 6   page 56 Dilemma Group C

Read the information about Fingertip. Make notes about the technology and its future market potential.

Fingertip is a new technology for opening doors without a key. People put their finger to a scanner beside the door. The system recognises fingerprints and opens the door for the right people. A group of scientists already have a design for the fingerprint scanner and they now want to set up a company to manufacture and sell it. The system costs about $300,000 to install.

Unit 7   page 66 Dilemma Group C

Read about Exeter. Which factors in the list in Task 1 does Exeter provide? Make notes and prepare to present your ideas to the class.

General:	Exeter is a beautiful historic city with a population of 113,000.
Economy:	Government is attracting new employment to the area. Businesses include: finance companies, banks, electricity.
Infrastructure:	Close to M5 motorway. London is two hours by rail. Small airport with destinations in the UK and some in Europe.
Commercial premises:	Modern business parks with high quality office premises.

Unit 8   page 74 Dilemma Group C: Kate

Good exam results – but not top class. Practical, not very academic.

Work experience: Before university, spent six months in Australia working in a hotel. Several different office administration jobs as a student.

Personality: Outgoing, lively and energetic, hard-working, ambitious. Likes working with people and being in a team. Dislikes routine tasks and working at a PC for long hours.

Career plan: Become a product manager in a travel company, setting up new tours, negotiating contracts and making key decisions.

Unit 9   page 82 Dilemma Group C: Hold a competition

Method:
Hold a competition in which students suggest ways to promote the brand to other students. The students with the best suggestions get the chance to put their ideas into practice and win an attractive prize.

Points to discuss:
How could you advertise the competition?
What prize could you offer that would attract a lot of students to enter?
What exactly should people do to win the competition?

Unit 12 page 108 Dilemma Group C: Offer higher pay

Current situation

House & Home offers low pay so the company doesn't attract good workers. Most workers are not very interested in the job and stay only a few months.

Possible good results: Staff work harder and may stay longer.

Possible bad results: Will cost a lot of money. You may not get the results you want.

Unit 10 page 92 Decision

EU Airlines share price trend

The best decisions were:

Buy 50,000 shares at the end of March.

Do nothing at the end of June.

Sell all shares at the end of September.

70,000 shares @ €3.50 gives you €245,000

Total value at December 31st = €245,000

Unit 14 page 120 Preview

Aquarium manufacturer

The solution was to use no packaging. The workers who transported the glass were much more careful and there weren't so many breakages. The company saved a lot of money on packaging, as well as the cost of replacing broken tanks.

Kinko's used their colour copying facilities to create individual calendars using personal photos. They make good Christmas presents and were very successful.

Unit 12 page 107 Student B

Situation 1: Supplier

Your company supplies vegetables to stores. You receive a phone call from a shop manager. Listen to the customer and offer two possible options:

1 – cancel the order and refund the cost.

2 – replace the order with a new delivery (they will receive it in about three hours).

Listen to the shop manager's decision and promise action.

Situation 2: Shop manager

Your shop sells bread. You ordered 200 rolls this morning but the supplier delivered 400. You can't sell 400. Phone the supplier, listen to the options and choose the best solution

Glossary

Unit 1   Activities

activity *n* [C] something that you do, or something that a company does: *The company has different activities, for example making computer games and videos.* Collocations *work activities, business activities*

diversify *v* [I] increase the range of goods or services a company produces: *Our company is diversifying into cosmetics* – diversification *n* [C, U]

employment *n* [U] work that you do to earn money: *After leaving university, I'm going to look for employment.* – employ *v* [T] to pay someone to work for you: *The company employs 2,000 people worldwide.* – employer *n* [C] a person or company that employs others – employee *n* [C] someone who works for another person or company

goods *n* [plural] things that a company produces for sale or for use: *Supermarkets buy goods and sell them to their customers.*

industry 1 *n* [U] the production of goods or services to sell: *Industry has become more competitive.* **2** [C] a particular type of industry or service: *The car industry is producing too many cars.* – industrial *adj*

manufacture *v* [T] produce large quantities of goods for sale using machinery: *Nike manufactures sports shoes.* – manufacturer *n* [C]

responsibility *n* [U] something that you are in charge of in a particular job: *The manager has responsibility for her department.* – be responsible for something *I'm responsible for telephone sales.*

retailer *n* [C] a business that sells goods to the general public and not to shops: *Dixons is a retailer of electronic goods.*

sector *n* [C] all the organisations or companies in a particular area of industry: *The number of jobs in the service sector is increasing.*

service *n* [C] usually plural] a business that sells help, advice, consultancy, etc., not manufacturing: *A lot of companies offer financial services now.*

team *n* [C] a group of people who work together to do a particular job: *We have an excellent sales team.*

Unit 2   Data

browse *v* [T] look for information on the internet: *About five hundred people browse our company website each day.* Collocation *browsing habits*

data *n* [U, plural] information or facts about a particular subject that someone has collected: *We don't have a lot of data on customers' buying habits.*

database *n* [C] an organised collection of information that is stored on a computer: *We are currently updating our customer files on the database.*

file *n* [C] a collection of information stored under a particular name on a computer, or in a box or paper cover: *Please check that the customer files are up-to-date.* – file *v* [T] – filing *adj* Collocations *computer files, filing system*

information technology abbreviation IT *n* [U] the study or use of electronic processes for storing information and making it available

record *n* [C] a piece of information that is written down or stored on computer so that it can be looked at in the future: *The sales team keeps a record of all customer enquiries.*

research *n* [C] serious study to find out new things about a subject: *Before we develop any new products, we need to do more research.* Collocations *conduct research, market research* – research *v* [T] – researcher *n* [C]

security *n* [U] feeling safe and free from worry about what might happen: *Cameras in the streets help to increase security.* – secure *adj* Collocations *security cameras, security staff, security systems*

store 1 *v* [T] to keep things in a special place until you need them: *You could store the paper in the photocopier room.* **2** *v* [T] to keep information on a computer or disk: *We store all our customers' addresses on the sales database.*

website *n* [C] a program on a computer that is connected to the internet, showing information about a particular organisation, company or subject: *You can find details of all our products on the company website.*

contact n [C] a person you know who may be able to help or advise you because of the work they do: *He has a lot of contacts in the film industry.*

etiquette n [U] the formal rules for polite behaviour in a group of people: *When you do business in a new country, it is important to be familiar with the etiquette.*

hierarchy n [C] a structure in which the staff are organised in levels and people at one level have authority over those below them: *The company president is at the top of the organisational hierarchy.* – hierarchical *adj*

organisation n [C] a company, business, group, etc. that has been formed for a particular purpose: *ANSI is an organisation in the US that fixes rules on the design of products.* – organisational *adj* – organise v [T]

punctual *adj* arriving at exactly the time that has been arranged: *She's always very punctual for appointments.* – punctuality n [U]

relationship n [C] the way in which people or groups work together: *We have a good relationship with our partners in the US.* Collocations *build a relationship, business relationship, develop a relationship, personal relationship, working relationship*

rule n [C] an official instruction that says how you should do things or what is allowed: *The phone companies are working under new rules now.*

status n [U] social or professional position in relation to other people: *Lawyers have high status in our society.* Collocations *high status, low status*

subordinate n [C] someone who has a lower position than someone else in an organisation: *I am responsible for six subordinates.*

working environment n [C] the general conditions in a workplace, including physical conditions (heat, light, noise, etc.) and relationships between people: *We have a very good working environment in our office.*

Unit 4   Image

advertising n [U] telling people publicly about a product or service in order to persuade them to buy it: *The cost of TV advertising is very high.* Collocation *advertising campaign* – advertise v [T] advertisement n [C] abbreviation advert, ad a piece of film, a picture or writing used in advertising: *I saw the advertisement in the newspaper yesterday.*

brand n [C] a name that a company gives to a product so that people can recognise it easily: *We built the Veuve Cliquot brand slowly over seven years.* Collocations *brand name, brand image* – branding n [U]

image n [C] the general opinion that most people have of a person, organisation or product: *Good advertising helps to promote a company's image.*

logo n [C] a design or way of writing the name that a company or organisation uses as an official sign on its products and advertising: *Nike uses a tick as its logo.*

loss leader n [C] a product that is sold at a loss to encourage people to buy other more profitable products: *Supermarkets sometimes sell bread as a loss leader to bring customers into the store.*

luxury n [C] something that is expensive and not really necessary, but pleasing and enjoyable: *The store sells luxury goods such as perfume.*

promote v [T] to try hard to improve sales of a product by advertising it, reducing its price, etc.: *They are promoting her new film heavily.* – promotion n [C] a special activity intended to sell a product or service

publicity n [U] the attention that a person or company gets from newspapers, television, etc.: *The show received good publicity in the media.*

target market n [C] a group of people that a product is aimed at; advertising of the product is designed to make the product appeal to this group: *You can't sell a product if you don't know the target market.*

value n [C, U] the amount of money something is worth – value for money of good quality, considering the price: *These jeans are good value for money at only $15.*

Unit 5   Success

bankrupt *adj* not having enough money to pay your debts and so not allowed to continue any business activities: *A lot of people will lose their jobs if the company goes bankrupt.*

business plan n [C] a document produced by a new company giving details of expected sales and costs, how the company can be financed and why it can expect to make money: *The bank needs to see a business plan before it will provide money for the start-up.*

company n [C] an organisation that makes or sells goods or services in order to make money: *He works for a software company.*

competition n [U] a situation in which businesses are trying to be more successful than others by selling more goods and services and making more profit: *There is strong competition between the two companies.* – compete v [I] – competitor n [C] – competitive adj

demand n [U] the total amount of a type of goods or services that people or companies want to buy: *There was strong demand for jeans last month.*

distribution n [U] the activities of making goods available to customers after they have been produced, for example, moving, storing and selling goods: *The company plans to use computers to improve distribution.*

entrepreneur n [C] someone who starts a company, arranges business deals and takes risks in order to make a profit: *She's a successful entrepreneur who has started several profitable companies.*

finance n [U] money provided or lent (for example by a bank) for investment in a business: *We need finance to start manufacturing our new product.* – finance v [T] Collocations *get finance, provide finance, raise finance*

loss n [U] when a business spends more money than it receives, or loses money on a particular deal or problem: *We had a loss of $20 million last year.* Collocations *make a loss, suffer a loss* – lose v [T]

market share n [C, U] the percentage of sales that a company or product has in a market: *The company hopes to increase its market share by 5 per cent next year.*

profit n [C, U] money that you make from selling something or doing business in a particular period, after taking away costs: *Coca-Cola reported strong profits last year.* Collocations *make a profit, earn a profit*

start-up n [C] a new company that has started to do business recently: *This bank specialises in providing finance for start-ups.*

Unit 6 Future

budget n [C] a detailed plan prepared by an organisation of how much money it will receive, how much it intends to spend and how it will spend the money: *The department has a budget of $4 million to spend on research.* Collocation *a tight budget* – budget v [I, T]

capital n [singular, U] money used to start a business: *You'll need more capital if you want the business to succeed.*

funding n [U] money which organisations, for example banks, lend to people and businesses for specific projects: [+ for] *Jane Hunter got funding for her business from venture capitalists.* Collocations *get funding, provide funding, raise funding*

funds n [plural] money that a person or organisation has available for a particular purpose: *Peter Jones is an entrepreneur with funds to invest in new business ideas.*

investment n [C] money that people or organisations put into a business in the hope of making a profit: [+ in] *Several rich people have made large investments in the space project.* Collocation *make an investment* – investor n [C] – invest v [I, T] [+ in]

joint venture n [C] a business activity in which two or more companies have invested together: *Ford and VW agreed a joint venture to build the Galaxy and Sharon models.*

launch v [T] to make a new product available for sale for the first time: *The company will launch a new model next month.*

payback period n [C] the period of time needed to get back the cost of an investment: *The payback period for space projects is very long.*

potential n [U] the possibility of future success of a product or venture: *No one wanted to invest in the project because they didn't think it had much potential.*

return on investment abbreviation ROI n [singular, U] the amount of profit on an investment in relation to the amount of money invested: *The project is risky and there may not be a good return on investment.*

technology n [U] knowledge dealing with scientific or industrial methods and the use of these methods in industry: *New technology gives us the possibility to explore space.* – technologies [plural] different types of technology: *The company is making use of different technologies to develop the new machine.*

venture n [C] a new business activity or project that involves taking risks: *The company is starting on a new venture to build small private aircraft.*

venture capitalist n [C] someone who invests money in new businesses: *Venture capitalists invested over $300 million in computer-related start-ups last year.*

Unit 7 Location

development 1 *n* [U] the growth or improvement of a business, industry or economy: *The government is providing funding for regional development.* **2** [U] planning and making new products or services: *The company is investing a lot of money in product development.* Collocation *research and development*

economy *n* [C] the system by which a country's goods and services are produced and used: *Europe's economy is expected to grow faster than the US.* Collocations *a strong economy, a weak economy*

employment *n* [U] the number of people in an area or country who have jobs, the types of jobs they have, etc.: *High employment is a key factor in a strong economy.*

growth *n* [U] an increase in the value of goods and services provided in a country or area: *Analysts are predicting strong economic growth next year.* – grow *v* [I] *The market grew slowly last year.*

inflation *n* [U] a continuing increase in the prices of goods and services: *The rate of inflation was 4 per cent last year.*

infrastructure *n* [C, U] the basic systems and structures that a country needs to make economic activity possible, for example, roads, communications, electricity: *The government invested €250 million in infrastructure.*

location *n* [C] the place where something is, especially a building or a business: *All the company's offices are in good locations.*

multi-national *n* [C] a large company that has offices, factories and business activities in many different countries: *It is difficult for small local companies to compete with the multi-nationals.*

region *n* [C] a large area of a country or of the world: *The north-east region is developing more rapidly than the south.* – regional *adj* Collocation *regional office*

unemployment *n* [U] the number of people in an area or country who don't have a job: *Since the factory closed, there has been high unemployment in the area.* – unemployed *adj*

Unit 8 Job-seeking

application *n* [C] a formal, written request for something – job application a formal request to be considered for a job: *We are considering your application for the job of marketing manager.* – apply *v* [+ for]: *He applied for the job of sales assistant.* – job applicant *n* [C] someone who is applying for a job

candidate *n* [C] someone that a company is considering for a job: *We are interviewing the candidates on Friday.*

career *n* [C] a profession or job you have trained for and intend to do for your working life, and which offers the chance to improve your status and salary: *I'm hoping to have a career in law.* Collocations *careers advisor, careers advisory service, change careers*

curriculum vitae abbreviation CV *n* [C] a document that gives details of a person's experience and qualifications: *It is important to prepare your CV in the right way.* Synonym *resumé AmE*

experience *n* [U] knowledge or skill that you have from doing a particular job: *He has years of experience in selling.*

headhunting *n* [U] finding a manager with the right skills and experience to do a particular job, often by persuading a suitable person to leave their present job: *We could ask a headhunting firm to find a new production director.* – headhunter *n* [C]

human resources abbreviation HR *n* [plural] the department in a company that deals with recruitment, training and helping employees: *He works in human resources.*

interview *n* [C] a formal meeting where someone is asked questions to find out if they are suitable for a job: *I have an interview for a job at Microsoft next week.* – interview *v* [T]

job *n* [C] the regular paid work that you do for an employer: *What's your job? I'm applying for a new job.*

qualification *n* [C] an examination that you passed at school, university or in your profession: *Candidates must have a university qualification.* – qualify *v* [I] – qualified *adj*

recruit *v* [T] to find new people to work for an organisation or company: *We're recruiting 20 new graduates this year.* – recruitment *n* [U]

salary *n* [C, U] money that you receive as payment for your work, usually every month: *The company offers good salaries.* Collocation *to earn a salary*

staff *n* [plural] the employees of an organisation: *A new manager is going to join the staff next month.* Synonyms *employees, workers.*

Unit 9 Selling

consumer *n* [C] a person who buys goods, products or services for their own use, not for business or to re-sell: *Consumers are demanding more choice and variety.*

customer *n* [C] a person or organisation that buys goods or services from a shop or company: *A customer telephoned this morning to ask about prices.*

direct mail *n* [U] advertisements that are sent in the post, often to people who are specially chosen because they might be interested in the product: *Over three billion items of direct mail were sent in the post last year.*

discount *n* [C] a reduction in the cost of a product or service, usually to encourage people to buy something: *We're offering a ten per cent discount on all furniture this week.* – discount *v* [T]

flyer *n* [C] a small sheet of paper advertising something. Flyers are usually handed to people or delivered to people's houses: *Let's use flyers to advertise the opening of our new store.*

marketing *n* [U] activities to design and sell a product or service by considering what buyers want or need: *We'll have to spend a lot on marketing to get customers back.*

sales *n* [plural] the value of goods and services that a company sells during a period of time: *Sales increased following our successful advertising campaign last year.*

sales pitch *n* [C] what a salesperson says about a product to persuade people to buy it: *The rep gave a ten-minute sales pitch about the new model.*

sales representative abbreviation **rep** *n* [C] a person who sells a company's products or services by speaking to customers on the phone or travelling to meet them: *He travelled all over the US as a sales representative.*

special offer *n* [C] a reduction in the price of something for a short time, to encourage people to buy it: *The company is running a special offer – a new phone for only £20.*

sponsor *v* [T] to give money to pay for a television programme, or sports or arts event, in exchange for advertising or to get public attention: *Mastercard is sponsoring the World Cup.* – sponsor *n* [C] a person or company that sponsors something – sponsorship *n* [U]

Unit 10 Price

cost 1 *n* [C, U] the amount of money that you have to pay to buy or produce something: *The cost of land in the city centre is very high.* **2** costs [plural] the money that a business must regularly spend in order to continue its activities. *Our profits are falling because of increasing costs.* Synonym *expenses n* [plural] Collocations *labour costs, manufacturing costs*

deal *n* [C] an agreement or arrangement, especially one that involves the sale of something to get a good **deal get** an agreement to buy or sell a product at a good price: *We got a good deal when we bought this office as demand was low at the time.*

graph *n* [C] a drawing that uses a line or lines to show the relationship between two sets of figures: *This graph shows sales figures for the year 2005.*

price *n* [C, U] the amount of money for which something is bought, sold or offered: *The price of this picture is £6,000.*

pricing *n* [U] the prices of a company's products in relation to each other and in relation to the prices of competitors; also the activity of setting prices: *We need to discuss our pricing if we want to boost sales.*

profit margin *n* [C] the difference between the price a product or service is sold for and the cost of producing it: *We can increase our profit margin by cutting the cost of production.*

share *n* [C] the ownership of a company is divided into shares, which can be made available for sale as a way to increase capital. Investors buy and sell shares in the hope of making a profit: *He made a lot of money by investing in IBM shares.*

spending *n* [U] the amount of money an organisation or a person spends: [+ on] *We need to increase spending on research and development.*

strategy *n* [C] a plan for achieving a goal; the best way for a company to develop in the future: *We need to develop a strategy for exporting the company's products.* Collocations *pricing strategy, develop a strategy* – strategic *adj*

trend *n* [C] the general way in which a particular situation is changing or developing: *Economists study the trends in spending.*

workforce *n* [C] all the people who work in a particular country, industry or workplace: *We are increasing our workforce from 1,200 to 1,400.*

Unit 11 Insurance

claim *n* [C] request for payment for damage, injury, theft, etc. for which you are insured: *If you want to make an insurance claim, you must fill out this form.* – claim *v* [T] [+ on] *He claimed for the damage on his car insurance.*

cover *v* [T] when an insurance policy covers someone or something, the insurance company will pay out if the person is injured; or if something is damaged, stolen, etc.: *The policy doesn't cover accidents that happen abroad.* – cover *n* [U] *The policy provides cover for loss, damage and theft.*

damage *n* [U] physical harm caused to something: *The fire caused $100,000 of damage.* – damage *v* [T] *The car was badly damaged in the accident.*

fraud *n* [U] a method of getting money illegally from a person or organisation often in a clever way: *Online banks need special software to protect against fraud.* – fraudulent *adj*

insurance *n* [U] an arrangement in which a company collects money regularly in premiums from a person or organisation, and in return agrees to pay them a sum of money if they are involved in an accident, have something stolen, etc.: *Travel companies recommend that their customers take out insurance.* Collocations *insurance claim, insurance company, insurance cover* – insure *v* [T] [+ against] *We are insured against fire and theft.*

insurance policy *n* [C] an insurance contract covering a particular risk, and the document that gives details of this: *In the policy, it says that we can claim up to £1 million for medical expenses.*

premium *n* [C] the amount paid for insurance during a particular period of time: *If you haven't paid your premiums, you will no longer be covered.*

risk *n* [C] the possibility of a particular type of damage against which you are covered: *Check in detail the risks that are covered by your policy.*

term *n* [C] one of the conditions of an agreement, contract or legal document: *According to the terms of the agreement, the company will pay within 10 days of accepting the claim.*

Unit 12 Service

apology *n* [C] something that you say or write to show you are sorry for doing something wrong: *The company sent an apology to their customers for their poor service.* apologise *v* [+ for + -ing] *We apologise for the inconvenience we have caused you.*

complaint *n* [C] a written or spoken statement by someone saying that they are unhappy about something: *Our sales assistants are trained to deal with customer complaints in a friendly manner.* – complain *v* [+ about] *Many customers have complained about late delivery.*

customer satisfaction *n* [U] when customers who have paid for a product or service feel happy with it: *Our main goal is to achieve customer satisfaction at all times.* – satisfied, dissatisfied *adj* [+ with] *We are very dissatisfied with the service at your hotel.*

customer service *n* [U] when an organisation helps customers by answering questions, listening to complaints, giving product advice, etc.: *The company says that it offers good customer service.* – customer services [plural] the department in a company that deals with customer service

feedback *n* [U] advice or criticism about products, services or ideas. Companies may seek customer feedback by providing questionnaires asking if customers are satisfied or not: *We conducted a survey to get feedback on customers' opinions about our products.*

guarantee *n* [C] a formal written promise to repair or replace a product if it has a fault within a period of time after you buy it: *The company offers a two-year guarantee on all electrical goods.* – guarantee *v* [T] *This product is guaranteed for two years.*

payment *n* [C] an amount of money that must be paid, or has been paid, or the act of paying it: *Payment must be made within 30 days.* – pay *v* [+ for] *Shoppers are willing to pay more for famous brands.*

quality *n* [U] used to talk about how good or bad something is: *Several customers complained about the poor quality of the service.*

refund *v* [T] to give someone their money back, for example, because they are not satisfied with the goods or services they have paid for: *We guarantee to refund your money if you are not fully satisfied.* – refund *n* [C]

training *n* [U] the process of teaching someone the skills and knowledge needed for a particular job: *The company is sending 30 workers to the US for training.* – train *v* [T] – trainer *n* [C] – trainee *n* [C]

Unit 13 Productivity

assembly *n* [U] the process of putting the parts of a product together in manufacturing: *Parts are manufactured in Japan and assembly is done in Turkey.* – assemble *v* [T] – assembly line *n* [C] method of making goods, especially cars, in a factory. The product moves along a line of machines or workers, each adding a different part or doing a different job.

capacity *n* [U] the amount of something that a factory can produce: *Our production capacity has increased with the new technology.*

component *n* [U] one part used in making a machine, vehicle, etc.: *The company supplies electrical components to the car industry.* Synonym part *n* [C]

delivery *n* [C, U] the act or process of bringing goods to the place or person who has ordered them: *We have arranged delivery of your order on Monday.* Collocations *just-in-time delivery, delivery date, delivery terms*

efficiency 1 *n* [C] how well an industrial process, factory or business works so that it produces as much as possible from the time, money and resources that are put into it: *We need to improve our efficiency if we want to become more profitable.* 2 how well and quickly a person works. – efficient *adj* – efficiently *adv*

just-in-time written abbreviation JIT *adj* if goods are produced or bought using a just-in-time system, they are delivered just before they are needed, which reduces the cost to the company of keeping goods for long periods of time Collocations *just-in-time delivery, just-in-time manufacturing*

production *n* [U] the process of making or growing things to be sold as products, usually in large quantities: *Toshiba is increasing production of its popular laptop computers.* – producer *n* [C] – produce *v* [T] – product *n* [C]

productivity *n* [U] the relationship between the amount of goods that a factory produces and the resources needed to produce them: *New technology has helped us to improve productivity.* – productive *adj*

resource *n* [C] [usually plural] this can include the money, buildings, machinery, materials, skills and workforce that a company has available: *The company doesn't have the resources to compete in a completely new market.* Collocations *human resources, financial resources*

stock, stocks *n* [C, U] a supply of raw materials or parts that have been produced and are kept to be used when needed in manufacturing, or a supply of finished goods that are kept before being sold: *It is expensive to store large quantities of stocks.*

supply *v* [T] to provide goods or services to customers, especially regularly over a long period of time: *The company supplies products to the car industry.* – supplier *n* [C] – supply *n* [C] [plural] supplies an amount of something that is available to be used: *We have a good supply of components in stock.*

waste *v* [T] to use more of something, especially time or money, than you need to, or to use it in a way that is not economical: *We waste too much time repairing old equipment.* Collocations *waste time, waste money, waste resources* – waste *n* [U]

Unit 14 Creativity

brainstorming *n* [U] a way of developing new ideas and solving problems by having a meeting where everyone makes suggestions and these are discussed: *The team held a brainstorming meeting to get ideas for selling the new product.*

challenge *n* [C] something difficult that you feel determined to solve or achieve: *The challenge for the company is how to pay its $3 billion debt.*

creative *adj* producing or using new and interesting ideas: *We need to find a creative solution to the problem of falling sales.* – creativity *n* [U]

discovery *n* [C] something you learn or find out that was hidden or not known about before: *Researchers have made some interesting discoveries about human thinking.* – discover *v* [T]

innovation *n* [U] the introduction of new ideas or methods: *The company encourages creativity and innovation.* – innovative *adj*

radical *adj* a radical solution involves looking at the original source of the problem and making big, important changes

solution *n* [C] a way of dealing with a problem or difficult situation: *There are no simple solutions to the problem of unemployment.* Collocation *find a solution* [+ for] – solve *v* [T]

tradition *n* [C] a way of doing something that has existed for a long time – traditional *adj*: *We need to move away from the traditional way of thinking.*

Unit 15   Motivation

bonus *n* [C] an extra amount of money added to an employee's salary for doing difficult or good work: *The sales staff get excellent bonuses when they reach their sales targets.*

initiative *n* [U] the ability to make decisions and take action without waiting for someone to tell you what to do: *Employees in our company are encouraged to use their initiative.*

job satisfaction *n* [U] a feeling of happiness or pleasure in doing your job or achieving something in your job: *Job satisfaction is just as important to workers as a bonus.*

loyal *adj* loyal employees stay with that company and don't seek jobs in other companies: *Martin has given 15 years of loyal service.* – loyalty *n* [U]

motivation *n* [U] willingness and enthusiasm to do something without being told to do it: *Many of our workers have little or no motivation.* – motivate *v* [T] [somebody to do something]

pay *n* [U] the money someone receives for the job they do: *The workers have asked for a pay increase.*

performance *n* [U] the way that someone does their job and how well they do it: *Some people criticised his performance as a manager.* – perform *v* [T]

power *n* [U] the ability or right to control people: *We shouldn't give too much power to one man.* – powerful *adj*

promote *v* [T] to give someone a better paid, more responsible job in a company or organisation: *The company has promoted him to the post of managing director.* – promotion *n* [C]

reward *v* [T] to give payment for excellent work, high performance or special service: *We like to reward our staff when they reach their production targets.* – reward *n* [C, U]

senior *adj* having a high position in an organisation or company: *Senior managers have their own office and drive a company car.* – seniority *n* [U]

Glossary test

1 We increased _____ on production and this has reduced our profit margin.

   A spending   B pricing
   C cutting   D output

2 Doug Richards is a successful _____ who has started a number of profitable businesses.

   A bankrupt   B loser
   C entrepreneur   D starter

3 When we had a fire, the insurance company paid the cost of the _____ .

   A policy   B cover
   C injury   D damage

4 Our regional _____ will visit you and show you our product range.

   A sales pitch   B sales representative
   C consumer   D customer

5 It was a difficult problem, so they had a _____ meeting to collect some ideas.

   A discovery   B brainstorming
   C challenge   D radical

6 This _____ shows the increase in oil prices over the last ten years.

   A workforce   B development
   C graph   D strategy

7 Venture capitalists look for a big _____ when they provide finance.

   A return on investment   B payback period
   C risk   D technology

8 If you need more information, _____ the company website.

   A browse   B collect
   C share   D store

9 Employees say that they get more job _____ when they are able to use their own initiative in their work.

   A pay   B satisfaction
   C loyalty   D seniority

10 To be sure of being polite to people, it is best to follow the rules of _____ .

   A contact   B etiquette
   C organisation   D relationship

11 Banks, financial services and consultancy businesses all belong to the _____ sector.

   A industrial   B service
   C manufacturing   D activity

12 The new product didn't sell well and the company lost _____ to its competitors.

   A distribution   B demand
   C market share   D finance

13 If you tell your insurance company that the value of your loss was higher than it really was, you are making a _____ claim.

   A fraudulent   B truthful
   C legitimate   D financial

14 The new technology is good, but the company needs a lot of _____ to develop it.

   A budget   B opportunity
   C potential   D funding

15 Supermarkets and other _____ sell goods directly to people who will use them.

   A employers   B teams
   C retailers   D manufacturers

16 The city is attracting lots of new business, which is good for economic _____ .

   A capital   B location
   C growth   D unemployment

17 We use a system of just-in-time _____ to reduce the cost of keeping large stocks.

   A orders   B efficiency
   C delivery   D productivity

18 Staff who stay with the company for longer than ten years receive an extra week's holiday as a reward for their _____ .

   A initiative   B performance
   C power   D loyalty

19 The _____ department has over 100 applications for the new position.

   A headhunting   B human resources
   C career   D staff

20 The bank is introducing a new surveillance system to increase _____ .

   A security   B files
   C browsing habits   D IT

21 Stefan _____ €5,000 from the insurance company after his car was stolen.

   A paid   B asked
   C claimed   D covered

22 The news story generated excellent _____ for our brand.

   A image   B publicity
   C logos   D loss leaders

23 When you have a meeting with new business partners, it is important to be _____ .

A late   B hierarchical
C punctual   D rude

24 Some of the items were damaged so the buyer made a/an _____ .

A apology   B refund
C complaint   D condition

25 Senior managers are responsible for their subordinates in the organisational _____ .

A status   B relationship
C hierarchy   D contact

26 I think we should offer a five per cent _____ to encourage people to buy more.

A offer   B flyer
C direct mail   D discount

27 _____ are people who have new ideas and think of new ways to do things.

A Traditionalists   B Innovators
C Researchers   D Transformers

28 We've reduced the price by 15 per cent, so the buyer is getting a good _____ .

A trade   B cost
C trend   D deal

29 Giorgio Armani is famous for creating a _____ brand.

A luxury   B value
C low cost   D cheap

30 We ask customers for their _____ to help us improve.

A dissatisfaction   B payment
C training   D feedback

31 Ferdinand is hoping to go abroad to work in one of his company's _____ offices.

A regional   B location
C capital   D zone

32 On the _____ line, the parts are put together to make the finished product.

A productivity   B capacity
C assembly   D supply

33 People on the trainee scheme have no work _____ , just a university qualification.

A CV   B experience
C application   D candidate

34 We'll have to _____ our products more if we want to sell more!

A design   B appeal
C brand   D promote

35 Our staff are important _____ which we try to use efficiently.

A components   B resources
C stocks   D deliveries

36 Several companies worked together on a _____ to launch the new satellite.

A potential   B risk
C joint venture   D venture capital

37 The team did a brilliant job so the company decided to _____ each of them with a large bonus.

A satisfy   B reward
C perform   D promote

38 John is _____ for a better job in a different company.

A hiring   B applying
C recruiting   D advising

39 We collect information about our customers and store it on a _____ .

A subject   B research
C record   D database

40 The economy is weak, with high _____ and unemployment.

A currency   B development
C infrastructure   D inflation

41 The product has a one-year _____ , so just bring it back if you have any problems with it.

A customer service   B refund
C guarantee   D apology

42 Bill Sorter, a finance manager, has _____ for a team of 12 accountants.

A diversification   B responsibility
C role   D activity

43 We _____ a football club, so our company name is on the players' shirts.

A sell   B sponsor
C offer   D launch

44 Advertising companies need good _____ staff.

A discovery   B traditional
C radical   D creative

45 Before you ask a bank for money, it is important to prepare a good _____ .

A business plan   B demand
C profit   D start-up

Grammar reference

Present simple and continuous

The present simple has the following uses.

- regular or routine events
  *We usually **start** the week with a team meeting.*
  *She **visits** Japan **once a month**.*
- permanent or long-term situations
  *I **work** at head office in London.*
  *The company **designs** computer games.*

> **Key words**
>
> *usually, normally, regularly, often, frequently, sometimes, rarely, always, never, every day / week / month / year, once a week / twice a month*

The present continuous has the following uses.

- something happening now / at the moment
  *Just a moment – I**'m trying to** find your file.*
  *Nick**'s talking** to a customer right now.*
- temporary situations
  *We**'re not developing** any new products this month.*
  *Eva**'s working** at home today – she's not in the office.*
- future fixed arrangements
  *We**'re flying** to Texas on Monday 19th.*
  *Mike**'s meeting** the directors tomorrow.*

> **Key words**
>
> *now, at the moment, currently, this week*

The continuous is not usually used with the following verbs.

- giving opinions
  like, dislike, prefer, think, believe, know, mean
- describing senses
  see, hear, feel, seem
- describing ownership and needs
  have, need, own, want

Countable and uncountable

countable nouns	uncountable nouns
have singular and plural forms	have no plural form
use *a / an* with the singular	never use *a / an*
use either singular or plural verb form	use only singular verb form
worker, book, desk, machine, coin, company, suggestion	*staff, oil, water, equipment, money, information, advice*

some

- in positive sentences
  – with countable nouns in the plural
  – with uncountable nouns
  *We're having **some problems**.*
  *There's **some coffee** on the table.*
- in offers and requests
  – with both countable and uncountable nouns
  *Would you like **some tea or some biscuits**?*

any

- in negative sentences and questions
  – with countable nouns in the plural
  – with uncountable nouns
  *We don't use **any videos** on our website.*
  *There isn't **any information** about hotels.*
  *Do you have **any details** about this?*

much

- mainly in negative sentences and questions
  – with uncountable nouns
  *We haven't got **much time**.*
  *Is there **much demand** in Europe?*

many

- mainly in negative sentences and questions
  – with countable nouns in the plural
  *Do you have **many customers** in the south?*
  *No, **not many**.*

a lot of / lots of (informal)

- in positive sentences
  – with countable nouns in the plural
  – with uncountable nouns
  *You see **a lot of surveillance cameras** in the streets in London.*
  *There's **a lot of computer crime** nowadays.*

Modal verbs

Form

- modal verbs are followed by the infinitive without to
  I **must go** now.
  I **can't find** the customer file.
  Could we **start** soon?

- exceptions are *have to* and *need to*
  I **need to go** now.
  We don't **have to keep** these records.
  Do you **have to leave** now?

Modals important for politeness

- offers
  Can I ... ? Could I ... ? I can ... I could ...
  Would you like ... ?
  Can I help you with your bags?
  Would you like to sit here?

- requests
  Can I ... ? Could I ... ? Can you ... ?
  Could you ... ? Would you ... ?
  Could I borrow your pen for a moment?
  Would you show me how to use this machine, please?

- polite suggestions
  You could ... / We could ...
  I think we should ...
  You could take the train – it's very fast.
  I think we should travel first class.

- permission
  Can I ... ? May I ... ? (more formal)
  You can / You may
  Can I / May I smoke in here? **Yes, you can.**

Modals of possibility

- certainty
  will / won't
  It's late – **I won't have time** to read the report tonight.

- possibility / uncertainty
  may, might, could, may not, might not
  We could have problems with transport.
  We may not arrive in time for the meeting.

Note: to express uncertainty in the future, we use *may not* or *might not*

We **may not / might not** make a profit next year.

- ability
  can / can't, could / couldn't (past)
  I can't read this. It's too small.
  I couldn't understand the report; it was too difficult.

Modals of obligation

- advice
  You should / You shouldn't ... (stronger)
  You must / You mustn't ... (very strong)
  You should talk to our accounts manager – she can help you.
  You mustn't leave London without visiting the Tower!

- personal rule   *must / mustn't*
  I must try to get to work earlier.

- general rule   *have to*
  Do you have to have a visa to travel to Russia?

- necessary   *need to*
  We need to plan our next sales conference soon.

- not necessary
  don't have to / don't need to
  You don't have to have a visa for the UK.
  You don't need to write a letter – you can phone.

- not allowed   *mustn't*
  You mustn't leave your car in front of the hotel – it's a no parking area!

Comparatives and superlatives

Forming comparative adjectives

- short adjectives (one syllable)   + -er
  The new model is **cheaper**.

- short adjectives ending -y   y̶ + -er
  The client is **happier** with the new design.

- longer adjectives (two or more syllables)
  more / less + adjective
  I think this coat is **more fashionable**.

- irregular comparative forms
  good – better
  bad – worse
  far – further
  The new design is **worse** than the old one.
  The other restaurant is **better** – but it's **further** away.

Use

- to show difference
  A is bigger **than** B
  B is **not as** big **as** A
  *The V8 is **faster than** the V6.*
  *The V6 isn't **as expensive as** the V8.*
- to show similarity
  A is **as** big **as** B
  *This year's sales are **as good as** last year's.*

Forming superlative adjectives

- short adjectives (one syllable) *the* + adjective + -est
  *This laptop is **the smallest** one on the market.*
- short adjectives ending -y
  (*the*) + adjective ~~y~~ + -iest
  *That was our **busiest** week of the year.*
- longer adjectives (two or more syllables) (*the*) *most / the least* + adjective
  *It's **the most beautiful** dress in the show.*
  *This is **the least expensive** model you can buy.*
- irregular superlative forms
  good – best
  bad – worst
  far – furthest
  *Which photo do you think is **best** for our advertisement?*
  *Arriving late is **the worst** thing you can do.*
  *My desk is the one that is **furthest** from the window.*

Past simple

The past simple has the following uses.

- events that happened at a definite time in the past
  *I **joined** the company in 2003.*
  *The new secretary **didn't come in** yesterday.*
- finished actions or events
  *When you **were** a student, **did you work** in the holidays?*
  *Yes, I **worked** for a telecoms company in the holidays.*
- finished time periods (with *for*)
  *Aisha **worked** in the finance department **for two years**, from 2003 till 2005.*

> **Key words**
>
> *in 2005, from 2002 to 2004, last week / month / year, yesterday, ago, in the past*

Future forms

will + infinitive has the following uses.

- predictions we feel certain about
  ***I'll definitely finish** this project tomorrow.*
  *We **won't have time** to look at your report this week.*
- intention, when we make the decision now to do something
  ***I'll let you know** what I decide.*
- intention after the verbs *think, hope* and *expect*
  ***Do you think you'll stay** with the company very long?*
  *We **hope you'll be able** to join the research team next year.*

going to + infinitive has the following uses.

- predictions we feel certain about
  *Are the staff **going to accept** the changes?*
  *It **isn't going to be** an easy meeting.*
  *It's **going to be** difficult to please everybody.*
- intentions, when the decision to do something was made before
  ***I'm going to visit** the Greek office next month.*
  *We **aren't going to stay** very long.*
  ***Are you going to stay** in Athens?*

The present continuous has the following use.

- arrangements for things to happen at a fixed time in the future
  *We**'re meeting** in the conference room at 10.*
  ***Are you seeing** the accountant tomorrow?*

The imperative

- positive instructions: infinitive of the verb without *to*
  ***Come** in!*
  ***Turn off** the lights when you leave.*
- negative instructions: *Don't* + infinitive without *to*
  ***Don't be** late!*
  ***Don't forget** to post those letters.*
- *Let's* + infinitive is also a polite imperative
  Let's finish.
  ***Let's go** for lunch now.*
- conditional instructions: *If* + present tense + imperative
  ***If you see** Joan, **give** her my best wishes.*
  ***Don't interrupt** him **if** he's busy.*
  ***If we don't get** an answer by Friday, **send** them another email.*

Present perfect

The present perfect has the following uses.

- recent events
  Sales figures **have improved** *recently.*
  We **haven't seen** *a big rise in demand.*
  Has *your manager just* **started?**
- events that affect the present situation (but we don't say when they happened)
  Prices **have gone up** *so they're very high now.*
- unfinished events starting in the past and continuing up to the present (using *for* and *since*)
  I've **been** *in sales* **since 1992.**
  The company **has been** *the market leader* **for three years** *now.*
- answering *How long?* about an unfinished event
  How long **have you worked** *for Exxon?*

> **Key words**
>
> *recently, in recent months / years, in the last month / year, just, now, since, for* (except with finished periods of time)

Passive verbs

Passive sentences are formed as follows.
Subject + *to be* + past participle (+ *by* + agent [person or thing who did the action])

Active: We **manufacture** the goods in Korea.
Passive: *The goods* **are manufactured** *in Korea.*

Active: The sales team **sold** 4,000 units last month.
Passive: *Four thousand units* **were sold** *last month.*

Active: The CEO **will open** the new factory next week.
Passive: *The factory* **will be opened** *by the CEO next week.*

The passive has the following uses.

- when we don't know who did something
  My purse **has been stolen!**
- when it isn't important who did something
  These products **were tested** *yesterday.*

- systems and processes
  Job applications **are sorted,** *and the best candidates* **are selected** *and* **interviewed.**
- formal language (letters and reports)
  Your enquiry **has been passed** *on to the sales department.*
  The market for DVD players **was researched** *last year, and the findings* **are reported** *in our December survey.*

Conditionals

Conditional instructions: *If* + present tense + imperative
If *I'm* **not** *in the office, please* **leave** *a message.*

Conditional 1
If + present tense + future with *will* or *won't*
If + present tense + *can / can't / could / couldn't*

If *our competitors* **find out** *about our new product,* **they'll want** *to copy it.*
We'll be *very happy* **if you can** *join us for dinner.*

Conditional 1 has the following uses.

- talk about the future results of a possible action or event
  If we spend *too much,* **we'll run out** *of money.*
  They won't buy *our products* **if they aren't** *good quality.*
  If *management* **doesn't give** *us the budget we need,* **we could have** *problems.*
- terms in a contract or agreement
  If you are not *fully satisfied with this product,* **we will refund** *your money.*

Conditional 2
If + past tense + *would / wouldn't*
If + past tense + *could / might*

If *the price* **was** *lower,* **I'd buy** *it.*
I **wouldn't buy** *it* **if it wasn't** *good quality.*
If *you* **reduced** *the price, we* **might be** *interested.*

Conditional 2 has the following uses.

- imagine unreal situations
  If *everyone* **used** *email,* **we wouldn't need** *to send letters.*
  If *electric cars* **didn't have** *so many disadvantages, more people* **would buy** *them.*

- imagine the results of improbable actions or events
  *If our sales increased by 15 per cent, **we'd make** a lot of profit.*
  *If **other companies entered** the market, there **would be** more competition.*

Adjectives and adverbs

Adjectives

- describe or qualify nouns
  *He's an **excellent** manager.*
  *The lunch was **delicious**!*

Word order

- in front of the noun
  *This is an **easy** task.*
- where there are several adjectives

size	colour	material	noun
a large	black	leather	bag

- after some verbs: *be, become, seem, feel*
  *The quality is **good**.*
  *The company is becoming **profitable**.*
  *I feel **tired**.*

Adverbs

- go with verbs to describe **how** you do something, or **how often** you do something
  *She **works efficiently**.*
  *I **often check** share prices on the internet.*

Adverbs that tell you how often: *sometimes, often, usually, rarely, occasionally, frequently, generally, normally, always, never*

Forming adverbs from adjectives

- most adjectives: + -ly
  slow – slowly
  large – largely
- adjectives ending in -y + -ily
  steady – steadily
- adjectives ending in -ic: + -ally
  automatic – automatically
- adjectives ending in -able: change ending to -ably
  reasonable – reasonably

- irregular adverbs

Adjective	Adverb
That's a **fast** car.	He drives too **fast**.
It's a very **hard** job to do.	The sales team is working **hard**.
They're **good** workers.	They do their job **well**.

Word order

- adverbs that tell you **how**
  – follow the verb
  – follow any object in the sentence
  *Sales rose **rapidly**.*
  *He spoke English **well**.*

- adverbs that tell you **how often**, as well as adverbs of **certainty and uncertainty**, can go:
  – in front of the main verb
  – between the first part of the verb and the main verb
  – at the beginning or end of the sentence

  *I **often work** till 6 o'clock.*
  *I **don't often travel** abroad.*
  *The price **will definitely rise**.*
  ***Sometimes** prices go down.*

Audioscripts

Part one

Many companies employ teams who work together across borders and time zones. We call them virtual teams because they communicate almost entirely by email. Modern technology makes communication very simple and fast – but there can be problems. There is a big risk of misunderstanding. With team members speaking different languages and belonging to different cultures, small problems can become big problems.

Part two

When you work together in a virtual team, you have to know and trust each other. It's important to build a relationship. When you join a virtual team, write an email to the others to introduce yourself. Tell your colleagues about your job, your work experience, your interests.

When you write an email, don't just focus on work. Make conversation – ask about the weather or mention something that is going on at the moment.

You need to explain things clearly to make sure there is no chance of misunderstanding.

If you have to say something negative, be careful. Remember, you can't smile in an email. A written message can sometimes seem very strong to the other person. Using polite phrases helps a lot!

When you often write to the same colleagues, you usually develop an informal, friendly style. But if you write to people in business that you don't know well, you need to be more formal.

Unit 1   **Listening 2** page 13

Olaf: I'm a systems developer and I work for a finance company. I'm responsible for our website and managing the IT systems. But I also develop new systems for the future.

Rania: I work as a project manager for a travel company. We help hotels to develop websites. My role is to meet clients and find out what they want from their website. Then I prepare a proposal and present it to them.

Da The: I'm a lawyer and I work for a mobile phone company. We make deals with companies to supply parts and services. My main role is to check the contracts with suppliers, but I also negotiate new contracts.

Jaana: I'm an accountant at a Finnish paper manufacturing company. We make the paper for magazines. I'm responsible for payments to suppliers. I check the invoices from suppliers and send the payments.

Unit 1   **Decision** page 14

Alistair Cross

George Johnstone is an excellent export manager and a very good salesman. But he doesn't have experience of Mexico. When you start to do business in a new region, it's very important to understand the culture. If you make mistakes, you can lose a customer. Linda has a lot of experience of doing business in Spain, and she knows something of South American cultures. She also speaks excellent Spanish. So we think that Linda is the best person to take responsibility for exports to Mexico. We know that she may not want to stay in the job for more than two or three years, so we are also looking for a new person to join the sales team – someone who speaks good Spanish and has a lot of experience of doing business in Latin America. Then if Linda wants to stop travelling, we will have someone who can take this role.

Unit 2   **Listening 1** page 16

Amy: Hello. I'm Amy. I work in the sales department and I manage customer data. I keep records of customers. We have a file for each customer with their name, address and order details. But I also store details about their buying habits. What are their likes and dislikes? How often do they order and so on. And I enter all this in the customer database. We use the information when we want to send special offers to different groups of customers.

Bob: I'm Bob and my job is to research the market. I try to answer three questions. One: how many consumers are there in the market? Two: who are they? And three: what do they want? We collect a lot of data about the people who browse our website. But we also use surveys and other methods. I write reports to help the marketing team develop their strategy.

Carla: My name is Carla. I work as a buyer. I always try to find the best products at the best price. Of course we have our regular suppliers. But I also search for new products, new suppliers and special offers on the internet. I use different search engines and I update our files with the new information.

Unit 2 **Listening 2** page 19

Bob: OK. Here is our weekly statistics report for our website. As you can see here, we had a total of 4,542 hits this week. That's very good – a lot more than we usually have. The average time for each session is 1.5 minutes. That's quite normal. And the average number of pages that people view in a session is 2.7. Again, nothing unusual there. The most popular page is the products page, with 2,430 hits. We expect this of course. Most people want to know about products. Then there's the offers page with 1,395 hits. We had a number of good deals on offer this week, and lots of people were interested in those! Now let's see the breakdown of traffic by continent. Most people who visit our website are from North America – that's 57 per cent. The Americans are usually top of the list, but this percentage isn't as high as last week. Then it's Europe with 31 per cent ... and after that ...

Unit 2 **Listening 3** page 19

1 a 815	b 10,000	c 4,905
2 a 3.2	b 10.98	c 15.361
3 a $\frac{1}{8}$	b $\frac{1}{3}$	c $\frac{2}{7}$
4 a 2%	b 48%	c 91.3%
5 a £102	b 4,000 USD	c €9m

Unit 2 **Listening 4** page 19

Sandra Ravell

Lots of people have to manage large amounts of information. You may be a manager, a secretary, or a student. When you have information that you may want to use in the future, you have to store it where you can find it again.

The first step is to decide how to structure your filing system. Ask yourself: What are the main categories of information that I deal with? Then divide them into sub-categories.

The second step is to create files for each kind of material. Give each file a name. Ask yourself: Is this name helpful when I want that file again?

The third step is to arrange your files for easy access. Ask yourself: Which files do I use often? Which are important? Put these files at the front of the filing area. Or on a computer, create a short-cut to those files.

Finally, keep your filing system up-to-date. Delete or throw away old material. File new information immediately in the right place. And review your system often. Ask yourself: Does this system work for me? Can I organise it better?

Finding information takes time. A good filing system can save you a lot of time.

Unit 2 **Listening 5** page 21

A Thanks for agreeing to help with my research.
B That's OK. What do you need to know?
A Well, first, about how many people are online, worldwide?
B Worldwide? It's difficult to say exactly. But we think it's about 600 million.
A Did you say 600 million? That's a lot!
B Yes. It's difficult to be precise because it's increasing all the time.
A Right. So how many of those are in Europe?
B About 30 per cent.
A Sorry – can I just check? Thirteen per cent?
B No, not thirTEEN, THIRty per cent.
A Thirty per cent. Hmm. So that's about 200 million.
B Just under 200 million, yes. The number I've got here is 190.91 million.
A What a number! Can you repeat it, please?
B A hundred and ninety point nine one million.
A OK. And how much time does each person spend browsing the web?
B The average time is over 25 hours.
A Do you mean 25 hours a week?
B No, no – 25 hours a month.
A Right, thanks. I think that's everything ...

Unit 2 **Decision** page 22

Deepak Gupta

Countries such as India and China have huge numbers of people and offer a great opportunity to companies like eBay. But there can be problems if you don't understand the local market. For example, people may shop in different ways and use different payment methods. There is also the problem of competition from local companies, for example Baazee, who have a better understanding of the market in India.

So what did eBay do? Well in 2004, eBay decided to buy the biggest online retailer in India – Baazee – for 50 million dollars. They believed that buying a local company was the best way to enter a new market. Baazee understood the market and could show eBay how to operate. Of course it was a high cost for the first year or two. But the company was sure that they would make money in the long term.

Unit 3   Listening 1 page 24

Part one

There are different opinions about what is polite or impolite. Different cultures express politeness in different ways. Even in the same country, there may be different views about what are good manners or bad manners. But the same rules apply everywhere. Politeness is about showing respect for others. It means thinking about other people's feelings.

Part two

In formal situations, we follow standard rules for politeness. In business, we are usually polite when we make new contacts, meet customers or people from other companies. Politeness is often linked to status. We are usually more polite to people above us in the organisational hierarchy. In today's working environment, most managers show respect for their workers. They might say, 'We really need to send the report as soon as possible. Could you please do it today?' If you consider other people's feelings, they are usually more willing to work hard, to help and to cooperate.

Unit 3   Listening 2 page 27

Sydney

We in Sydney are very easy-going and relaxed about rules. But we work hard. We start work pretty early in the morning. Breakfast meetings are common, starting at 8am. And we like to start meetings on time – so it's important not to be late! We're generally very informal. Men often wear a jacket and tie during office hours. But we prefer informal clothes when the weather's hot. For lunch, we usually go out for a sandwich. What do we talk about? Well – it isn't difficult to talk to Australians – we're very friendly people. But it helps a lot if you can talk about sport.

London

Most people that I know don't like to start work early. We hate breakfast meetings! People are always in a hurry – so being on time for meetings is important. People think the British are very formal. But things are changing. I think we're quite informal nowadays. Some men still wear formal business suits – but a lot of people come to work in casual clothes. Lunch is often a quick sandwich and a coffee. After work, we like to go to the pub with colleagues. At the pub you can talk about anything you like!

New York

Life in New York is fast and dynamic. Some people say that we're rude. I don't mean to be rude – I just don't have much time for being polite! Work starts early in the morning – breakfast meetings start at 7am – don't be late! Most people dress in suits for business – it's important to look smart. A lot of people eat at their desk at lunchtime. But if we go to a restaurant, we talk business right through lunch. We don't talk about the food. People are very competitive and work always comes first!

Unit 3   Listening 3 page 28

1 Could you give me your coat, please?
2 Could you give me your coat, please?
3 Could I have some more coffee, please?
4 Bring me that document, please.
5 Mary! Can you go and find some more chairs.
6 Would you sign this form, please?

Unit 3   Listening 4 page 29

Conversation 1
John: Excuse me, there's a mistake – my name is J – O – H – N, not J – O – N.
Jane: Oh, OK.

Conversation 2
Jack: Would you like to come with us to a restaurant for dinner this evening?
Barbara: That would be very nice. Thank you!

Conversation 3
John: Can I introduce Caroline Day?
Barbara: Oh – we already know each other. Hello, Caroline! How are you?

Conversation 4
Jack: Is it OK to park in front of the office?
Jane: I'm sorry. It isn't allowed. You can use the car park at the back.

Conversation 5

Jane: Thanks very much for the gift. It's beautiful!
Barbara: I'm glad you like it.

Conversation 6

John: Thanks for all your help with the travel.
Jack: That's all right. No problem.

Unit 3 Decision page 30

Gary Robinson

Bullying is a difficult problem and the solution depends on the situation and the type of bully. In Elizabeth's case, she is the only one in her team that Valma bullies. This probably means that Valma sees Elizabeth as a competitor and that's why she tries to make her look stupid. She wants to keep her at the lowest level in the team.

Elizabeth should not try to talk to Valma directly. This will only make things more difficult between them.

The best option for Elizabeth, therefore, is to talk to a senior manager. But first, she must collect as many facts as she can. It is a good idea to keep a diary of events. Each time she experiences bullying, she should make a note of it, writing down where and when it happened. If her colleagues can support her story, that's even better. If the senior manager understands the situation, he can move Elizabeth to another team or to another department. Or he may decide to move the bully. He can also give Elizabeth the chance to do the training she wants.

If the senior manager doesn't believe Elizabeth, or doesn't want to help her, then the only solution for her, unfortunately, is to leave the company. Bullying causes a lot of stress. It's better to start again in a new job than to continue in a bad situation for months or years.

Unit 4 Listening 1 page 36

luxury	luxurious
fashion	fashionable
industry	industrial
creation	creative
commerce	commercial
economy	economic
fame	famous
talent	talented

Unit 4 Listening 2 page 37

Dee Delaney

Companies don't just sell products. They sell a lifestyle. Nearly everything you buy says something about you: your clothes, your car, your mobile, all show what kind of life you have. Customers choose brands that represent their lifestyle, or the lifestyle they want to have.

Through advertising, companies try to promote an image of the kind of people their customers want to be. For example, Ray-Ban – the sunglasses producer – ran an advertising campaign with photos of strong, dynamic men. The idea was that men who are leaders and heroes wear Ray-Bans.

Another example is Gap. They have a range of clothing for men called StressFree. You can drop something on your trousers and it cleans off immediately. So you have no worries. You can be relaxed and stylish at the same time. The company advertised the clothing with the song, *I'm Free*.

Unit 4 Listening 3 page 39

Customer 1

I think it's a good desk. You can use it for a PC or laptop. I'm a student and I need a desk to study. I could put it in my bedroom. The desk is quite small, so it's ideal for a small room. But it's got lots of space for books and papers. It's great, yeah!

Customer 2

I'm an office designer and it's part of my job to choose desks and chairs for new offices. In my opinion, this desk isn't designed for use in an office. It's too small. Most office workers need more space. When you have to sit at a desk all day, you need a bigger desk than this!

Customer 3

I have an office job but I also work at home. I think this desk could be suitable for me. It looks stylish. It's made of good quality wood. And I like the fact that it's got wheels – so you can move it easily. I think it's very practical.

Unit 4   **Decision** page 40

Ernst Jungbaum

To solve its problem, VW launched two new models: the Touareg, a top-end sports utility vehicle, and the Phaeton, a luxury executive car. Although their business up to that time was based on middle-priced cars, they knew that there was very good business in the luxury car market too. They wanted to give their existing customers something to move on to.

They also wanted to build some of the best cars in the luxury market and be a strong competitor just as they were in their existing markets. It isn't easy to develop a new image – it takes a little time. But the company felt sure that the time was right to make the move.

Unit 5   **Listening 1** page 42

Jake Goldrick

What makes a company successful?

To begin with, of course, a successful company has to make a profit. That means that it has to keep costs as low as possible – the cost of manufacturing, for example. Secondly you need to make big sales so there has to be a demand for your products. And of course, you want to be competitive. If your competitor brings out a better product, you can lose customers. The most successful companies control the market. That means they have a bigger percentage of sales and a bigger market share than their competitors. Their product is market leader. It sells more than any other product in that sector.

Another factor for success is growth. No company wants to stand still. Successful companies are always finding new markets and new opportunities to grow.

Unit 5   **Listening 2** page 45

Alan Martin

Well the first step, of course, is to develop a new product idea. Many people decide to start a business because they have a good idea.

But you have to remember that about 80 per cent of new business ideas fail. Usually it's because people don't understand the market. So the second step is to conduct market research. Your research should answer two key questions. First, is there a demand for your product or service? Second, who are your competitors?

When you know you have a market, the next step is to prepare a good business plan. Your business plan helps you to focus on what you want to do. It also helps with the fourth step: getting finance.

You have to decide what type of business you want to have, your goals, your product or service and its key selling points. In the plan, you also need to show that you can run the business. So you include information about staff, management, production, marketing and, of course, finance. This shows that you know how to run a business.

But the most important step is the fifth one: to build a customer base. You need a number of regular customers who come back to you year after year. A strong customer base is key to making a success of your business.

Unit 5   **Listening 3** page 47

Ben Hope

After graduating, I joined a design company. It was a good job and I enjoyed it. But only **two years later**, the company went bankrupt and I lost my job. I looked for other jobs, but couldn't find anything interesting. **So what did I do?** I decided to start my own business. **To begin with**, it was very hard work. But **after about a year**, I got my first big contract: to design the new offices of a local company. The company liked what I did and I got more work. **Then** came economic problems. It was a difficult time for all businesses in the region. But **after a while** the economy improved again and my business started to grow. **And now** I employ 12 people and we work in luxury offices in the city centre.

Unit 5   **Decision** page 48

Ronald Dean

We first considered Golden Valley. This is already a successful company and very profitable. But the owners of Golden Valley had no reason to sell. They were already so successful that they didn't need any financial help from a larger company.

We also considered Rocky Farm because they had such an excellent product. But they only had one product: ice cream. It needed a lot of money and time before it could develop into a bigger business. We wanted to find a firm that could become market leader in a short time.

So, our decision was to make an offer for Annie's Kitchen. This firm had financial difficulties and its owner was ready to accept a low offer from us. Because we are a big company, we were able to deal with the company's financial problems. We paid for a new factory and put money into improving production. So Annie's Kitchen started to make a profit. The owner stayed on as the company's managing director. This worked out very well. Annie's Kitchen is now second in the market with a 32 per cent share. We hope that we will soon be number one!

Unit 6 Listening 1 page 53

Christoph Wiesenthal

Questioner: What kinds of new technology does your firm usually invest in?

Christoph: Mostly we invest in IT – Information Technology. But about a third of our capital is invested in medical technologies.

Questioner: Is it better to support start-up companies or older companies?

Christoph: Obviously there's a lot more risk with a start-up than with a company that is already running. With an older company, you can see if they have a strong management team and a good record of success.

Questioner: When you consider new projects or new ideas, what do you look for?

Christoph: We look for new products and new technology that will have a large market. If it's something people need to have, then lots of people will buy it. Take a medical product, for example. We ask what kind of disease it will treat. If it can treat a disease that is common, obviously, the product will have a much larger market.

Questioner: Many people who look for venture capital are scientists or engineers. How much do they understand about business?

Christoph: Nowadays, top scientists know a lot about business. They are very aware of the importance of economic factors.

Questioner: How long do you usually have to wait to get a return on investment?

Christoph: The payback period is usually between five and eight years. But in the biotech sector, 15 years is quite normal.

Questioner: And – if I can ask you this – what percentage of your investments don't give you any return on your investment?

Christoph: Venture capitalists expect that nine out of ten ventures won't make any return. If all goes well, the tenth investment will make enough money to give us a profit overall.

Unit 6 Listening 2 page 55

John

People are worried about the amount of garbage they create. This idea offers people a way to manage garbage. But it'll be quite expensive! So I think it'll probably sell only in the luxury market.

Jemima

Maybe at first it will only sell in the luxury market. But in the long term, I think the price may come down. By 2020, the Intelligent Garbage Can could be in every home!

Jim

It's a great product idea! It will solve all our garbage problems! This will definitely be a big success!

Jo

Sorry – I don't think so. It's a toy for people who like technology and have too much money to spend. It won't solve garbage problems. I don't think it will sell – not in any big numbers.

Unit 6 Decision page 56

Christoph Wiesenthal

Let's look at the space travel idea first. It's true that there are people who would love to be space tourists. But how many people will be able to pay $30,000? There'll be a very small market for this. And it's also the riskiest venture of the three. The company will need huge amounts of capital to build a spacecraft that is safe. So at the end of it all, there may not be much return on investment.

OK, let's look at Fingertip next. This is a great idea. One day, this kind of system will be in homes, offices – everywhere. But at present, you can only sell it to luxury hotels and big corporations. So, in the short term, the market will be very small. There is also a greater risk here because it's a new start-up.

So, finally, let's look at Celf Cure. This is something we are very interested in. We know that the technique can be used to treat several common diseases. That means that there will definitely be a big demand for this kind of treatment. There is also less risk investing in this business because it's an existing company so we know they have the necessary management skills to develop the idea. We think this venture will be a big success. That's why we've decided to invest our capital in Celf Cure.

Unit 7   Listening page 63

Declan Murphy

Before setting up an office in another country, you'll need to do quite a lot of research. There are a number of things to consider.

To start with, you want to be sure that the country has a strong economy. And that means low inflation and a stable currency. If the prospects for growth are good, then so much the better.

Then you need to consider other factors. For example, does the location have a good infrastructure – a modern airport, good roads and perhaps shipping facilities if you need them?

And the third main area to research is the financial side. How much will it cost to rent office space? Does the government of the region offer special encouragement to foreign business such as low taxation? If the local government has a positive attitude to foreign business and the costs are low, then obviously these are going to be big advantages.

Unit 7   Decision page 66

Charles Jerome

There are three key elements in deciding where to locate a new office. The first is the infrastructure of the area. Do you have good road and rail communications? Are you near to an international airport?

The second key element is the living environment. You need to offer staff an attractive place to live where they can find a nice house that's not too expensive, and good education for their children.

The third element is the business environment. A place that has a growing economy with other successful businesses in the area will provide the best environment for your company.

So which of the three towns did Whiterose choose? Well, they considered Exeter because it offers a very attractive environment. But it is a long way from London and head office. Communications to other parts of Britain are not so easy and international travel is not as good from Exeter airport as from other larger airports.

They considered Swindon because it has excellent communications with the rest of Britain and is not too far from Heathrow – a huge international airport. But Swindon is mainly a manufacturing town and doesn't have other similar businesses in the service sector. So perhaps it isn't the right business environment for a hotel company.

So they decided that they are going to relocate to Luton. Luton has a growing economy and the airport is attracting airline business and travel companies to the area. Whiterose may want to work together with some of these companies. Luton may not be such an attractive place to live as Exeter, but it *is* close to London. The staff could travel from London in half an hour, so maybe it won't be necessary to move house. Luton also has excellent communications with the rest of Britain and internationally. Staff can fly to many places around the world from their local airport, which is a big advantage for a company that is expanding internationally.

Unit 8   Listening 1 page 68

Michael: I'm Michael Kohl and I work for Volkswagen in the design department. I work on the exterior design for new cars, making models for the design ideas. When I left school, I applied to do an apprenticeship with Volkswagen. I thought it would be a good company to work for. So I wrote to them to apply for the scheme. I was one of 6,000 applicants for only 600 places. After a lot of tests and interviews, they accepted me. After three years in the apprenticeship, I went to a special college to study design and modelling. When I got my qualification, Volkswagen gave me a permanent job.

Sanjay: I got my job through personal contacts. I was on a two-year master's degree course in management. A family friend had a job with Meridian, a management consultancy firm and she told me about it. I was looking for a summer work placement to get experience and she recommended me to the managing director. I learned a lot working there and enjoyed it very much. After I finished my degree, they decided to hire me. And that's where I work now – as a research consultant.

Barry Hampton

If you apply for a job in the UK, it may be better to write your CV in the way that UK employers expect. For example, keep it short – don't write more than two pages.

Make sure that you put your personal details and qualifications at the top – where you studied and your exam results. Don't write your date of birth and don't say if you are married or not.

When you describe your work experience, it's essential to say what you learnt from your previous jobs. Say what you contributed to the job, and what skills you demonstrated.

It's a good idea to write something about yourself and any interests or hobbies that you have. And don't forget to say which foreign languages you can speak.

Finally, remember to give the contact details of two references – most British employers will contact them to find out more about you.

Unit 8   Decision page 74

Barbara Kingsland

As a careers adviser, I never say to anyone: you must take this job or that one. It has to be their decision. We carry out psychological tests that show what kind of personality people have, what their strengths and weaknesses are. This helps them to know what kind of work they are suited to.

Kate, for example, likes working with people not machines. The job in the small company may suit her very well. But one thing to think about is risk. Kate could lose her job if there is a downturn in the industry.

She will probably find the market research job a bit boring. But if she is really ambitious, it may be better to take a job with a large company that offers good prospects in the long term.

It is important for Kate to think about her long term plans. That will help her to make the right decision.

Kate Gray

It's now three years since I decided to join Wide World Tours. I think it was a good decision. I didn't much like the job of marketing assistant – it was a bit boring and routine. But I worked hard and the company gave me the chance to move to the Human Resources department. I'm now taking a year out to study for a Human Resources qualification. Then I'll go back to Wide World Tours to continue my career. Because it's a big company, it offers lots of opportunities!

Unit 9   Listening 1 page 76

Mario Capelli

Perhaps the most effective way to promote products to a large number of people is to advertise. There are several different advertising media that we can use, for example TV and radio. There's also the press – that's newspapers and magazines – and the cinema. And of course, the internet is extremely important now. Advertising is a good way to reach a lot of potential customers – but there are other selling techniques as well.

There's personal selling, for example. This means employing sales representatives to make regular sales visits to customers and potential customers.

Then there are sales promotions. These include special offers, for example: 'Ten per cent reduction in price'; or 'Buy satellite TV and get free installation' and discounts that encourage people to buy.

Other examples of sales promotions include competitions and free gifts.

Another method of promotion is public relations. This involves creating news and getting information about the company or its products in the press or on TV. For example, when a pop star launches a new album, people write about it in the music magazines. And this brings publicity for the company.

The next method is direct marketing. This includes all sales activities where consumers can buy the product immediately. An example is direct mail – where you send information to potential customers by post. We can also include TV and internet shopping in this category. And then there's telephone selling, where sales staff telephone people and try to sell products over the phone.

And finally, we have sponsorship. A company pays money to have its name linked to an event or a person such as a sports personality. The person wears clothing with the name of the company on it.

Michio Yano

We know our customers very well, and we decided that a trade fair wasn't the most effective way to launch our new modem. Instead, we wanted to create a fun event that our customers could remember for a long time – a party.

The way we promoted the event was this. We sent several emails to our customers. In the first email, we encouraged the customers to visit our website to see a Flash demonstration of the new product. Next, we emailed invitations to the launch party. We later sent another email so that they couldn't possibly forget. The third email included directions to the event.

We chose a big hotel by the beach and we arranged special buses to make it easy to attend. We organised lots of games and entertainment to make the party really good fun. During the event, we used big screen TVs to provide more information about the product. People could watch demonstrations on the TV screens and enjoy the party at the same time.

The event was a huge success. We planned for 250 people to come, but 600 people came. Many people said it was the best launch party ever!

Speaker 1: How about putting up some posters? We can put posters up in the store so people can see them when they come in.
Speaker 2: That's a good idea! – And why not hand out leaflets as well? We can put one in each bag when a customer buys something.
Speaker 3: Hmm – I like that! And of course, we need to put details on our website.
Speaker 1: Perhaps we could collect customers' contact details – their home address or email address – then we could send them information about the classes.
Speaker 2: Hmm – I'm not sure about that! People won't want to give their address.
Speaker 3: You're right. That could be difficult. I think we should just have posters and leaflets.
Speaker 1: What about inviting someone from the press to attend the first class? That way we can get some free publicity!
Speaker 2 and 3: Brilliant!

Nikki Lambert

At Virgin Mobile, we believe it is very important to have students inside each university, helping us to promote our brand. One of our strategies is to recruit two student brand managers at each university. These students carry out promotional work and receive pay for each hour of work. We advertise the jobs on our special student website. Students can apply online and we select the most talented applicants through tests and interviews. We don't just accept anyone who shows an interest – it's important to use standard recruitment procedures to select people who have a real talent for marketing. We also give these recruits two days of special training in marketing methods. So this is one strategy. But we also have another: a competition which we hold every year. The prize is a house where each winner, and three of their friends, can live rent free for a year. We advertise the competition on the internet. But the student brand managers also do a lot to encourage people to enter. The first stage of the competition is to complete an online personality test to see how dynamic and creative they are. In the second stage, they have to describe an idea for promoting Virgin Mobile. We then select the best 25 students to go on to the third stage. In this stage, the students have to persuade other students to vote for them to win. This means they have to promote themselves in some way. For example, they can put up posters, get attention at student events by wearing special clothes, dye their hair red, hold parties, decorate the town in red or anything else they can think of. They do these activities to promote themselves to win the competition, but of course they are also promoting the Virgin brand at the same time. And this is an extra benefit to our marketing campaign. We find that this competition attracts a lot of interest from students who want to become involved. And this is great for increasing familiarity with our brand. We are also offering something to students: a lot of fun, and the chance to save on some of their living costs at university.

Callum Taylor

Part one

Price is important to everyone. Companies spend a lot of time deciding how to set prices. But they often don't choose the best method of pricing their products. This can have a huge impact on profitability. A study of 2,400 companies showed what happened when they followed one of three strategies. The first strategy was to reduce costs by one per cent; the second was to increase the volume of sales by one per cent; and the third was to increase all their prices by one per cent. The companies who reduced their costs improved profitability by 2.3 per cent. The companies who increased their volume of sales also had an increase in profitability – of 3.3 per cent. But the companies who increased their prices saw the biggest increase, with profits increased by as much as 11 per cent.

Part two

So how should companies set the price for a product? One method is a simple 'cost-plus' strategy. You calculate what it costs to produce an item and then you add the profit margin you'd like to have. And that's your price.

Another method is to find out what your customers are ready to spend on that product. Then you set the price to match.

And a third way is to look at the competition. You see what your competitors are asking for the same kind of product and you set your price at about the same, or lower if you want to be competitive.

Pricing is really difficult to get right and companies have to think carefully about the different factors. For example, ask: Who are your target customers and is price important for them? A second question is: What kind of product or service are you selling? Because if it's a quality product or a special service that no one else can offer, then asking a lower price won't help your sales. Pricing should be part of your plan. You shouldn't develop a product and then say: 'OK, now let's think of a price.'

Presenter 1

Graph A shows the company share price over the first six months of the year. As you can see, the share price has increased from 95 cents in January to 105 cents in June.

Presenter 2

Graph B shows changes in the price of oil during the last year. As you can see, the price has fluctuated between 30 and 40 dollars a barrel.

Presenter 3

Graph C shows the average cost of renting an apartment between 2000 and 2005. As you can see, the cost reached a peak of 150 euros a square metre in 2001. More recently, the cost has fallen.

Presenter 4

Graph D shows the average cost of travel between London and Paris over a five-year period. As you can see, the cost fell to a low point in 2003. But in the last year, it has gone up.

Presenter 5

Graph E shows the rate of inflation over the last three years. As you can see, the rate has remained steady at 3.5 per cent during this period.

Task 1

March

It's March 31st and it's 6pm. EU Airlines reports losses over the last three months of 45 million euros. The company has debts of 3 billion euros and ticket sales are falling. This is partly due to a downturn in the world economy, and partly due to competition from low cost airlines. Frank Petit, the airline's CEO, has announced today that the company is planning to cut costs. Four thousand people will lose their jobs over the next year. The share price rose to one euro eighty in January, but has since fallen, and stands at one euro per share today.

June

It's June 30th and it's 6pm. EU Airlines reports an increase in profits over the last three months. Thanks to a programme of cost cutting, profits for the quarter reached 63 million euros. However, the airline's workforce are planning strikes in protest against job cuts. These strikes will cause problems for passengers which could result in a fall in ticket sales. The share price has risen over the last three months and reached a peak of two euros at the beginning of June. But news of the planned strikes has pushed the price down again and today it stands at one euro sixty per share.

September

It's September 30th and it's 6pm. EU Airlines reports a big rise in profits over the last three months, reaching a total of 125 million euros for the quarter. Passenger numbers have increased substantially to Asia and the Pacific, North and South America, the Middle East and Africa. Only numbers within Europe remain low because of competition from low-cost airlines. The company has solved its employee relations problems and the strikes planned for the summer did not take place. The share price has increased over the last three months and has reached three euros fifty, the highest level for the year so far.

Task 2

December

It's December 31st and it's 6pm. EU Airlines has reported a fall in profits over the last three months, from 125 million euros in the third quarter to just 65 million for the fourth quarter. The recent rise in oil prices has put pressure on the airlines to increase fares. As a result, passenger numbers have fallen. And strikes at three major airports during a holiday weekend in November meant that many passengers were not able to fly. The share price has fallen by more than a third in the last quarter and currently stands at two euros.

Unit 11 Listening 1 page 95

Part one

Interviewer: Can you explain how an insurance company is structured?

Irene: Well, we have three main departments: life products, commercial insurance and private insurance. Each department has a manager who is in charge of the staff and takes care of general administration. Each department also has clerical staff, who answer the phone and deal with online applications and claims. They handle most applications and claims. But when there are special cases, they bring them to the underwriters, who are experts on the products handled by that department. When there is a question about an application for insurance cover, the underwriters make the decision to accept or decline the risk.

Part two

Interviewer: What do you mean by 'special cases'?

Irene: Well, for example, if someone is applying for insurance, on the application form we ask the question: 'Have you made any previous claims in the last four years?' When someone has made three claims or more in a four-year period, we see that person as 'high risk' and we don't really want to offer them cover. But there may be cases where we can review the situation. For example, a customer who made several claims for theft lived in an area of high crime. But perhaps he has now moved to a new address in a district with less crime. So we can review his case. Sometimes we agree to accept the risk but with special terms and conditions. We may quote a higher premium or offer only limited cover.

Unit 11 Listening 2 page 99

Irene

The fact is, it's company policy. We don't insure people with a criminal conviction. He has a criminal conviction, so we can't offer him insurance.

Jane

I understand your point, but he was convicted 20 years ago! He hasn't done anything wrong since then. Don't you think we should review the situation?

Mike

On the other hand, we don't know that he hasn't done anything wrong. Maybe he simply hasn't been caught by the police.

Jane

Yes, but it's also possible that he's now an honest person. And in that case, our policy is unfair.

Irene

Surely the main point is that he has been dishonest. My view is that we shouldn't take the risk. He could be dishonest again.

Mike

That's right – you have to consider the risk. In this case, the risk is too great.

Carl Herring

The insurance company's view was that Jane did not take reasonable steps to prevent the theft. The problem is to decide what the 'reasonable steps' are. Did Jane act in an unreasonable way? No one told Jane to replace the locks of her car. She reported the theft of her handbag to the police and her insurance company – but she was not given any advice about changing the car's locks. So the insurance company couldn't expect her to know that it was her responsibility. Jane did replace the locks on her house – which costs about €80. On the other hand, the cost of replacing the electronic locks on a car is nearly €1,000. It wasn't reasonable to do this on an old car. So our ruling in this case is that the decision was unfair and the company should settle the claim.

Customer service trainer

It is very important to be polite and helpful at all times, and to see things from the customer's point of view.

If a customer is very angry about a mistake, stay calm. Don't get angry yourself. You may think: 'I didn't make the mistake. This isn't my responsibility.' Dealing with customers' complaints often means solving problems that aren't your fault. The answer is to solve the problem professionally as part of the job.

When the customer explains the problem, listen carefully and repeat to check that you have understood. Often the customer just wants to express his feelings. If he doesn't demand any action, you'll have to suggest a solution.

Sometimes you can't do exactly what the customer would like you to do. In this situation, you have to say what you can do. It is essential to use the right language. You will give the customer more confidence if you say: 'I will'; not 'I might' or 'I can't'. Don't say: 'I don't think we can do that', say: 'I will find out for you'.

Of course there are times when you just can't win. For example, if it's a very difficult person who will not cooperate, then you probably won't find a solution. But you'll know that you have done your best. You have to try to provide your customer with what he or she wants.

Shane: OT Components. How may I help?
Magda: Good morning. This is Magda Zawadski from Fortuna in Poland. We recently ordered some components and I'm afraid we've got a problem. We ordered 15 but you sent 50!
Shane: Oh! I'm sorry about that. How many have we charged for in the invoice?
Magda: You charged for 50. And unfortunately, we have paid by automatic payment. So it means we have paid too much.
Shane: Yes I see. Well we've got two options. I can either send you a credit note, or I can request the accounts department to refund your money. If you are ordering from us again, it'll be easier to send you a credit note. If I arrange a refund, you'll have to wait three to four weeks before you receive it.
Magda: Well, we probably won't order from you again for two to three months. So it's better if you refund the money.
Shane: OK. That's no problem. I'll arrange that for you. And I'll also ask our distributor to collect the extra units that you don't want.
Magda: OK, thank you very much.
Shane: I'm sorry about the mistake. Please accept our apologies.

Mandy Dunwoody

We had to make some difficult decisions. We decided not to recruit more staff but to try to keep the staff we have and improve staff training. This was essential because customer feedback told us that our customer service was poor. So we increased the training programme for new workers from one day to two days. We also introduced a weekly training session in each store. This has helped to develop service skills and to keep staff up-to-date with new information about products.

We also increased staff pay levels. We offered a 3 per cent pay increase to everybody. But because we had a problem keeping staff for a long time, we offered a 5 per cent increase to staff who stayed more than one year. We also offer bonuses to people who show the most enthusiasm and the best customer service skills.

We are very pleased with the results of our decisions. Our customer service has improved, our customers are happy, and more of them come back to shop in our stores again.

Interviewer + Paul Gardner

I   Is productivity an important concept in your business?

P   Yes, it is. When you increase productivity, you reduce costs and increase your profit. And all businesses are trying to increase profit.

I   How have you increased productivity?

P   Mainly by investing in new equipment that uses up-to-date technology and does the work more efficiently. But experience is also vital. We started in 1986, and we have learnt a lot. We've improved our methods and learnt how to solve problems.

I   What kind of problems?

P   Well as we're a chemical plant, it's technical problems, mainly. If there's a problem with the process, it will produce a poor quality product which we can't sell and we lose a lot of money. Mistakes can be very expensive! But people are the biggest problem – managing people.

I   Why is that?

P   Well, if there's a lot of work to do, people don't always agree to work overtime, especially if it's at night. Or people may be sick and then we are short of staff.

I   Is it a problem to find good workers?

P   It's very difficult. So when you've found good people, you want to keep them. We've been very successful in keeping our staff. Most have been with us for more than ten years. They have a lot of experience and they all work well as a team. That's essential to high productivity – good teamwork!

Gavin Floyd

My job is to improve productivity by trying to maximise the use of resources. In our company, we use a system called 'Six Sigma' which many companies use to improve productivity. The system helps us to create a plan of the production process from raw materials to finished goods. We collect data about each stage, and the system analyses the data. This may show that we are wasting time or resources on something that isn't essential, so we cut it out. We may cut out part of the production process, or we may reduce the use of some materials. We're trying to save costs on anything that isn't absolutely essential to production or to the product. Six Sigma helps us

to reduce every kind of waste – wasted time, wasted resources and wasted energy.

Extract 1

A   I know this isn't on our agenda today, but could we quickly talk about holidays?

B   OK – but we're running out of time, so can you please keep it short?

Extract 2

B   Does anyone have any other questions about the schedule?

Others   'No' 'That's OK' 'Fine'.

B   It's time to finish. Thank you all for coming.

Extract 3

B   OK. Let's start. We don't have much time this morning because the inspectors are coming and we must finish by 11 o'clock. So, have you all seen the document I sent you?

George Mann

We decided to reduce the targets for the productivity bonus to make it easier to earn a bonus. We thought it would make people work harder and we expected that better productivity would follow. In fact, the decision was a disaster. It made things worse, because workers still failed to meet production targets and their morale fell even lower. In the end we had to ask Patrick Massey, the old production manager, to come back to the company. He was a strong leader and very popular. He didn't want his old job back so we offered him a position on the board of directors. The workers were happy to see him back and morale improved immediately. Roland Court decided to leave and Patrick helped to recruit a new production manager who could do the job efficiently. At last productivity has started to improve again and we've learnt that good leadership and good people management are absolutely essential to high productivity.

Example   ec<u>o</u>nomy   econ<u>o</u>mical
1   imagi<u>na</u>tion   im<u>a</u>ginative
2   compe<u>ti</u>tion   comp<u>e</u>titive
3   <u>a</u>ccident   acci<u>de</u>ntal
4   inno<u>va</u>tion   <u>inn</u>ovative
.

Interviewer + Paul Saunders

Part one

I   In what fields of business is creativity especially important?

P   Every business. People think that creativity is only important in marketing, or advertising. But it's just as important in engineering, for example. In today's business world, there's a lot of competition so you have to do something different – something no one else is doing.

Part two

I   How can companies be different?

P   It's the people in the company who make the difference. Your competitors can copy your products, but they can't copy your people.

I   Are some people more creative than others?

P   The old thinking was that only some people are creative. But everyone can be creative – just in different ways. There are two types of people. Adaptors are careful and realistic. They look after the details. They are important for making improvements in the day-to-day running of the business. For example, they may find ways to reduce product faults. Innovators are people who want radical changes. They like to challenge the normal way of doing things and are happy to take risks. These people are important to a company when things are changing. But they're not team players and they usually hate meetings. So it may be hard for them to work together with the adaptors.

I   What can managers do to stimulate creativity?

P   People can only be creative in the right environment. It's essential for managers to encourage their staff to make suggestions and be ready to try new things. To be a creative leader, you have to take risks and accept the possibility of failure.

Part one

Speaker 1: Well, I can only see three solutions. Reprint the brochure, fire the person responsible, or print labels with the correct number. What do you think of the first idea?

Speaker 2: We can't reprint two million brochures. The cost would be much too high. If we did that, we would use all our marketing budget for the next two years!

Speaker 1: OK. What about the second idea? Fire the person responsible?

Speaker 2: Maybe! But it wouldn't help.

Speaker 3: It wouldn't solve the problem.

Speaker 1: And the third idea – to print labels with the correct telephone number?

Speaker 2: That would work. But we'd have to stick them on each brochure. It would take a long time!

Speaker 3: And it wouldn't look good. It would be obvious that we'd made a mistake.

Speaker 1: What we really want is a good brochure with no mistakes and no extra cost! What else could we do?

Part two

Speaker 3: OK. Let's look at this another way. What if the number was correct?

Speaker 1: But it isn't correct. What do you mean?

Speaker 3: What if we contacted the telephone company and asked them to change the number?

Everyone: Ah!

Speaker 1: That could be the solution! Brilliant!

The gold mining company, Goldcorp, has discovered gold at its Red Lake mine in northern Ontario. The new discovery contains high grade gold ore and could make Goldcorp the richest gold mine in the world.

CEO Rob McEwen, shocked the industry recently when he held a competition for the world's geologists to help him find gold. Mr McEwen put details of the area's geology on the internet and offered prize money to anyone who could suggest the best place to dig for gold. More than 1,400 entries were received from scientists around the world. The judges were surprised at the creativity of the competitors, who had never visited the mine and carried out their research using only computer models. The top prize of $105,000 went to a group of geologists from Australia whose work led to the new discovery. The results have been a spectacular success and the Red Lake mine is now producing 504,000 ounces of high grade gold per year.

Unit 15 **Listening 1** page 128

Dilys Breeze

Motivation means different things to different people. Some people are motivated by money and competition; others are motivated by working in a friendly environment, or being able to have fun.

Most people feel motivated when they know they are making a contribution, and doing something useful. People need to receive praise. They want to feel that others listen to their problems or suggestions. And most want to develop their skills and learn new things.

It's important for managers to stimulate and encourage their staff to get the best from them. Staff will be more motivated if they have a challenge, and the work is interesting. But they also need to believe that they can do the job. So it's important for managers to support their staff, listen to their problems and help them feel more confident. People only get satisfaction from work if they feel they can do it well.

Unit 15 **Listening 2** page 132

Clark Morris

To feel motivated, workers have four kinds of needs called the four Cs. The first C is connection. To feel connected to the company, people need to understand their role and feel that they are helping to achieve the company goals. The second C is content. Workers need to enjoy the job in order to get satisfaction from it. The third C is context: the company's systems and organisation. This can include the IT network, machine maintenance, or the pay system. If things don't work smoothly – because the computer system is out-of-date, for example – workers will soon become demotivated because they can't do a good job. The final C is climate, or company culture. It depends on the relationships between management and staff. In order to create a good climate, managers need to listen to the staff and respond to their suggestions. They should encourage staff to have ideas and use their initiative, and support their team when they need help. Employees may feel angry or stressed if the climate is poor. So it's very important to create a good climate. Companies should pay close attention to these factors so that their staff will be more productive.

Unit 15 **Listening 3** page 133

Interviewer + candidate

1
I: Why did you leave your previous job?
C1: Because the pay wasn't very good, so I decided to look for something better.

2
I: Why did you leave your previous job?
C2: Because it wasn't a challenge any more. The job was the same every day, so there was nothing new to learn.

3
I: Why have you applied for this job?
C2: So that I can learn something new and develop my skills.

4
I: Why have you decided to change your job?
C3: The company I work for at the moment is very small. That means that the career prospects aren't very good.

5
I: Why have you applied for this job?
C3: In order to improve my career prospects. This is a bigger company, so I think I'll have more opportunities.

Unit 15 **Decision** page 134

Kok Tan Hiang

When we moved, we changed our office design. We built larger working spaces where people could sit together. We only needed work spaces for two-thirds of our staff, so hot-desking was the obvious solution. We also wanted to create a more democratic workplace. We wanted better communication between people at all levels.

Was it a good decision? Well, hot-desking was a good solution for us. We already had the technology to implement the new working arrangements. Many of our staff, such as sales and technical teams, like the hot-desking arrangement. They have a dynamic environment to work in and it helps them to be more creative. However, we had to make permanent work spaces for people who were dissatisfied with the new arrangement. The lawyers, for example, needed permanent space to store books. In the business world of today, you have to be ready to change. Fortunately, most of our workers adapted easily.